STEPHEN PLATTEN

CATHEDRALS OF BRITAIN

An imprint of B. T. Batsford Limited

Written by Stephen Platten.

Pictures reproduced with kind permission of David Iliff, CC-BY-SA 3.0, except for the following: Shutterstock: 1, 5, 9, 12, 13, 19, 20, 30, 31, 48, 56, 72, 78, 79, 88, 89, 91, back cover bottom.
Getty: 11 top, 90.
Alamy: front cover, 29 top, 59, 84.

Edited by David Salmo and Charlotte Mozley

ISBN: 978-1-84165-875-9

2/23
Printed by Leo Paper Products, China

Pitkin Publishing
Batsford Books
43 Great Ormond Street
London WC1N 3HZ

www.batsfordbooks.com

Front cover: Exeter Cathedral.
Back cover: Ely Cathedral (top),
Durham Cathedral (bottom).

Previous page: Stained-glass, Lincoln Cathedral.
Right: York Minster Choir.

CONTENTS

Lady Chapel, Ely Cathedral.

INTRODUCTION

Journeying across Europe, how might one begin to define a medieval city? It's as likely as not that one might begin with the cathedral and the 'cathedral quarter' which often nestles around the great church. Cathedrals invariably sit at the heart of historic cities and, in England, it is often assumed that the status of a city is assured by the presence of its cathedral. Strictly speaking that is not the case. In Lancashire, for example, Blackburn, with its cathedral remains a 'town', whereas nearby Preston, with no cathedral, has been granted a charter as a 'city'.

Nonetheless, cathedral and city frequently evolve together and even the smallest cathedral locations often sport the name city locally, as for example with Southwell. So, across Europe, cities will be remembered by the distinctiveness of their cathedrals. Salamanca in Spain is unique with its old and new cathedrals adjoining each other like Siamese twins. The compact central German city of Bamberg has at its heart an unusual cathedral with stepped apses at either end. Florence is identified by the dome of its Duomo and Milan by the myriad pinnacles of its cathedral church. Chartres is perhaps best of all known for its treasury of stained glass.

Salisbury Cathedral's vast lawns.

England too brings its own character. Few English cathedrals have the closely packed precinct which is so common in France; Truro is possibly the most notable exception with the church tucked into its centre. But more characteristic of the English pattern is the 'close', often an extended and sometimes walled precinct with more open space. Salisbury is surrounded by vast billiard-table-like lawns. Norwich's close is a village within the city's heart; Norwich shares with Wells its own water gate. Lichfield and Peterborough are each set within a compact, almost islanded close. Gloucester's close protected the cathedral from the growing nineteenth-century industrial incursions. Lincoln stands astride its broad 'Minster Yard', proudly majestic on its prominent cliff. Durham has retained so much of its former monastic infrastructure and Canterbury's precincts include splendid ruins alongside the great monastic cathedral building itself. So essentially 'English' are these locations assumed to be that even a brand of cheese has gained its reputation by being described as 'Cathedral City'.

But even within Britain, cathedrals are not unique to England. The six Welsh Anglican cathedrals all have medieval, and indeed earlier, roots. St Davids and Llandaff are again placed within the wider expanses of a precinct. Bangor, St Asaph's and Newport are more focal within their towns or cities. Brecon carries something of each of these. In Scotland, the complexities of the Reformation have left a more 'mixed economy', and nowhere are there the exact equivalent of English cathedral closes. But the magnificence and glory of the buildings remains in common, from St Mungo's in Glasgow in the south to the cathedral of St Magnus in Kirkwall, far north in Orkney. More modest, but architecturally attractive are St Ninian's, Perth and the Cathedral of the Isles. St Giles' High Kirk, Edinburgh and St Machar's, Aberdeen retain the craggy majesty of Scottish ecclesiastical architecture.

THE BISHOP'S CHURCH

Cathedrals take their name, of course, from the 'cathedra' or bishop's throne, which stands at their heart. A cathedral is thus the church of the bishop, the focus of his teaching authority. Early on, cathedrals would have been basilical in form, that is oblong with an apsidal (semi-circular) end. At the centre of this semi-circle sat the bishop, flanked by his college of advisers, teaching his assembled flock. In Norwich, the eastern cathedra preserves this pattern, at the heart of a 'basilican' presbytery. Over the centuries the pattern of cathedral building evolved and many of them became cruciform (cross-shaped) in plan. Often this came about through association with a monastery. In England particularly, many of the cathedrals in the Middle Ages were administered by Benedictine monks: Worcester, Canterbury, Peterborough, Durham, Ely, Gloucester, Winchester, Carlisle and Norwich are examples. In these cathedrals it was the 'prior' who ran the monastery; the bishop, who lived in separate accommodation, was de facto the monastery's abbot. Other English cathedrals were secular from the beginning with a college of canons at their heart. Such was the case in York, Lincoln, Hereford, Chichester, Salisbury and St Paul's in London.

ARCHITECTURAL DEVELOPMENT

The style of architecture of English cathedrals and abbeys developed just as did the communities who inhabited them. The simplicity of Saxon architecture, often with fairly primitive round-headed arches and windows, gave way to the austere strength of the Romanesque style. Romanesque took its name from the solid round arcades and strong pillars which had developed from Roman architecture. In England this style is primarily associated with the Norman invaders and is often simply styled Norman. Durham Cathedral and Tewkesbury Abbey are two good examples from this period. St Albans, a cathedral only since the late nineteenth century, displays the earliest Romanesque, almost halfway between the earlier Saxon style used in the original abbey on that site.

In the late-Romanesque period the arches began to become pointed and this style is often termed Transitional. In the late twelfth and early thirteenth centuries, Romanesque gave way to the lighter touch of Early English, focused on the familiar three slender and parallel lancets seen at Rievaulx, at Whitby, and in the soaring elegance of Salisbury Cathedral. Early English marks the beginnings of medieval English Gothic, which matured into the intricacy of the Decorated and Geometric tracery familiar in so many English parish churches. Among cathedrals, York Minster is a splendid example, as is the nave of Beverley Minster. The apotheosis of English Gothic is reached in the Perpendicular period, during the fifteenth and sixteenth centuries, with its strong vertical lines and sumptuous fan-vaulting. Early fourteenth century displays of this style of vaulting can be seen in the cloisters at Gloucester and Wells. St George's Chapel, Windsor, and King's College Chapel, Cambridge, are perfect examples. The nave of Canterbury Cathedral is another magnificent expression of the Perpendicular style.

Canterbury Cathedral's Perpendicular nave.

The Renaissance led eventually to the rediscovery of the principles of Classical architecture, and the seventeenth and eighteenth centuries saw a flowering of the Classical style. The small city centre cathedrals in Derby and Birmingham are built elegantly in this manner and Wren's rebuilding of St Paul's in London is the most triumphant example of this style. In the nineteenth century, medieval Gothic was revived: Truro Cathedral, the Anglican cathedral in Liverpool and even the smaller Roman Catholic cathedral in Oban are each effectively born of this rediscovery of medievalism, albeit in a most creative manner. In some ways, even Guildford and Coventry owe something of their origins to a modernised or transformed Gothic. Modernism has led to a far greater freedom of expression, and different routes have been followed. The Roman Catholic cathedrals at Brentwood, at Clifton in Bristol, and at Liverpool testify to this variety, and it is to this myriad mixture of architectural styles and expression that this book seeks to introduce you. Among the Welsh medieval cathedrals are many similarities; in Scotland there is a greater independence of style, although both St Mungo's, Glasgow, and St Giles', Edinburgh, were influenced by the Gothic of northern England.

Above: St Paul's Cathedral, London.
Opposite: Chester Cathedral.

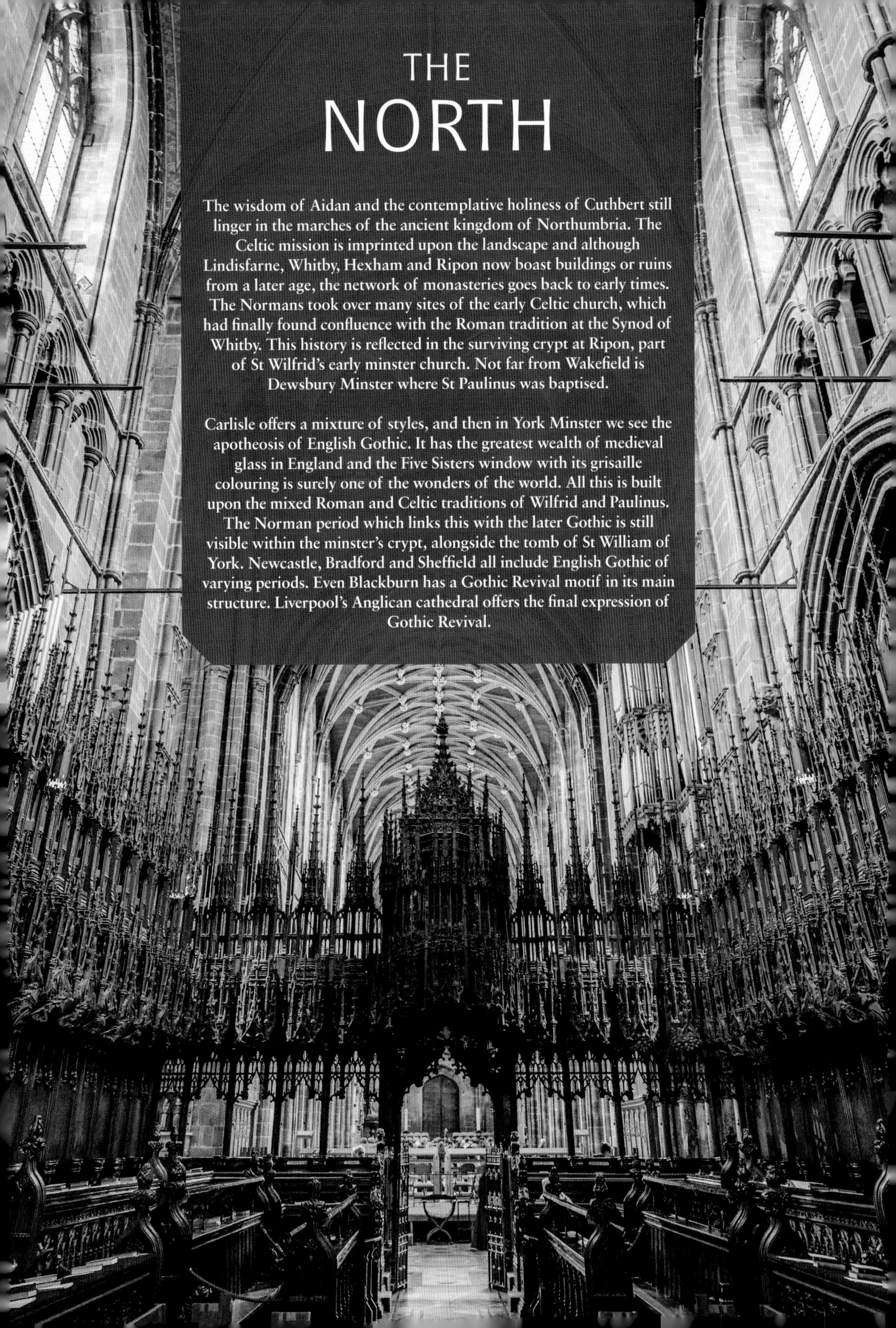

THE NORTH

The wisdom of Aidan and the contemplative holiness of Cuthbert still linger in the marches of the ancient kingdom of Northumbria. The Celtic mission is imprinted upon the landscape and although Lindisfarne, Whitby, Hexham and Ripon now boast buildings or ruins from a later age, the network of monasteries goes back to early times. The Normans took over many sites of the early Celtic church, which had finally found confluence with the Roman tradition at the Synod of Whitby. This history is reflected in the surviving crypt at Ripon, part of St Wilfrid's early minster church. Not far from Wakefield is Dewsbury Minster where St Paulinus was baptised.

Carlisle offers a mixture of styles, and then in York Minster we see the apotheosis of English Gothic. It has the greatest wealth of medieval glass in England and the Five Sisters window with its grisaille colouring is surely one of the wonders of the world. All this is built upon the mixed Roman and Celtic traditions of Wilfrid and Paulinus. The Norman period which links this with the later Gothic is still visible within the minster's crypt, alongside the tomb of St William of York. Newcastle, Bradford and Sheffield all include English Gothic of varying periods. Even Blackburn has a Gothic Revival motif in its main structure. Liverpool's Anglican cathedral offers the final expression of Gothic Revival.

CARLISLE CATHEDRAL

Carlisle Cathedral has seen perhaps greater ravages from a tempestuous past than most cathedrals; the truncated nave is the most obvious evidence of this. More cryptic evidence of its place on the frontier between England and Scotland is in its stones used originally either in Hadrian's Wall, or in the wall of the Roman city. All this adds to the cathedral's uniqueness, which is enhanced by it being the only medieval monastic cathedral to have been set within an Augustinian rather than a Benedictine priory.

Viewing the cathedral before entering it, it is easy to appreciate something of its history. King Henry I founded the Augustinian priory and church of St Mary in 1123. In 1133 he carved a new diocese of Carlisle out of the See of Durham and within ten years of its foundation the priory church became a cathedral. From the beginning it was cruciform in plan. The remains of the nave are part of the earliest Romanesque building, constructed by Bishop Athelwold, the first bishop. The central tower was rebuilt by Bishop Strickland between 1400 and 1419.

The nave, converted into the chapel of the Border Regiment by the architect Stephen Dykes Bower in 1949, contains fine Romanesque arcading. The missing four and a half bays were demolished during the Puritan Revolution between 1649 and 1652. The transepts are also Romanesque; the north transept forms St Wilfrid's chapel and includes the Brougham triptych, carved in Antwerp around 1510. Moving into the choir, the architecture becomes Gothic. After a fire in 1292 destroyed much of the arcading, the remaining work was retained and supported by new piers. The splendid Decorated great east window parallels similar work at York Minster and Selby Abbey. The fifteenth-century stalls in the choir are very fine; on the backs of the stalls in the south aisle paintings tell the story of St Augustine, and in the north aisle, that of St Anthony and St Cuthbert.

Good evidence of the former monastery remains, in the Prior's Tower, Gatehouse, Tithe Barn and in the noble refectory (fratry) which became the Chapter House in the seventeenth century. In October 2018, the Fratry Project began. A cloister-style building at the south-west corner of the cathedral will make the ancient fratry more accessible and provide new hospitality facilities.

Viewed from the south west.

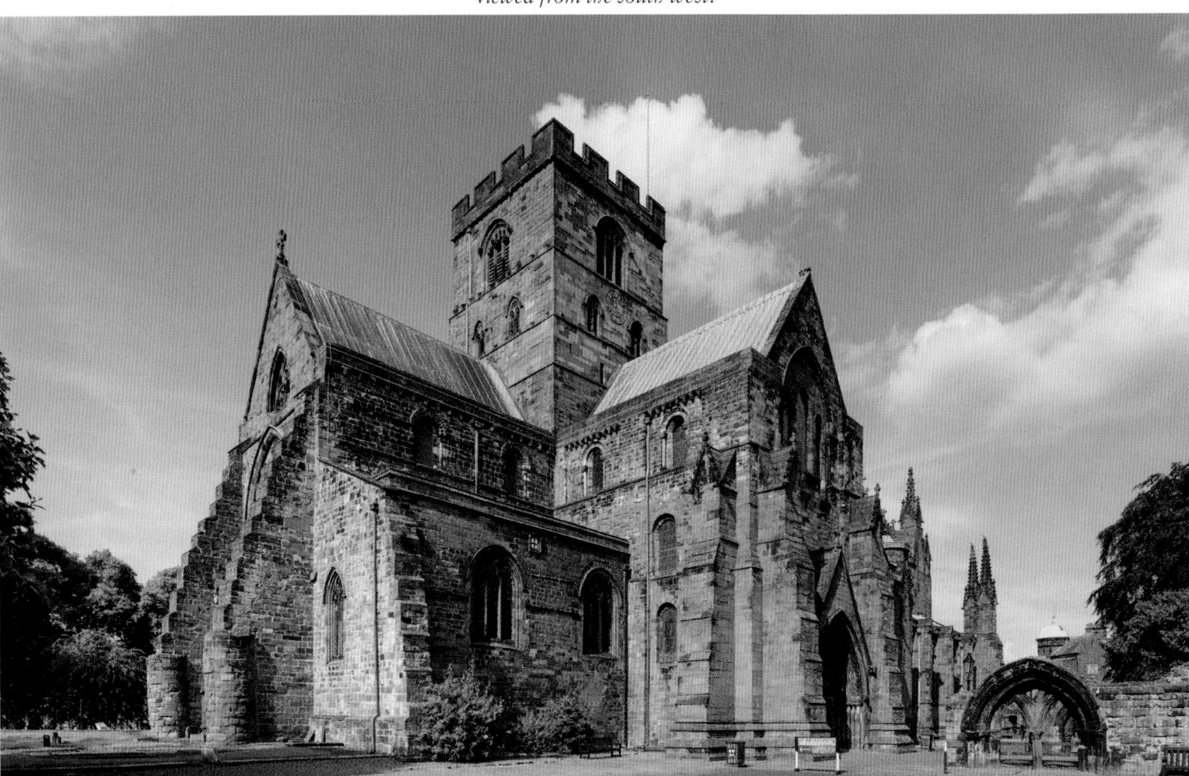

NEWCASTLE CATHEDRAL

Of Newcastle's medieval past, the two most prominent surviving features are without doubt, the castle keep and the nearby striking crown spire of St Nicholas' church, which, since the creation of the diocese in 1882, has been the cathedral. The crown spire was the inspiration later on for that of St Giles' High Kirk in Edinburgh.

The massive crossing piers owe their origin to the rebuilding of the church in the fourteenth century when nave and choir were constructed. In the north and south transepts, the south aisle and clerestory windows are part of the original Decorated period.

The ingenious design of the crown spire dates to 1435–70. Blackett's library of 1736 is notable. The fine organ case is by the celebrated London organ builder, Renatus Harris. The superb Perpendicular font and cover (depicting the Coronation of the Virgin) are from *c.* 1500.

Amongst other treasures is Tintoretto's painting of Christ washing the disciples' feet. The delightful Maddison memorial in the south transept depicting Henry and Elizabeth Maddison and their 16 children is the pièce de résistance. Stephen Cox's Eucharistic sculpture is on the rear of the reredos wall. The planned removal of the pews will create a greater sense of space and light; alongside the internal work, the western churchyard will be landscaped making the cathedral more obviously welcoming to all.

Left: The medieval crown spire.

BRADFORD CATHEDRAL

Just to the north of Bradford stands the ancient parish church of St Peter. With the foundation of the Diocese of Bradford in 1919, St Peter's became the cathedral. The nave, which is the oldest part of the building, was completed in 1458 and the oak roof resting on splendid painted angels was added in 1724. The gritstone tower in Perpendicular style was finished by 1508.

The font stands at the crossing of the entrance aisles at the west end of the cathedral; its cover is a spectacular piece of Perpendicular with a crocketed spire, sitting on a series of buttresses with fine tracery. Edward Maufe (also the architect of Guildford Cathedral) was commissioned to extend the cathedral between 1952 and 1965. These additions are in simplified Gothic.

The cathedral is blessed with some fine wall tablets including those to the Lister family. Joseph Priestley, the notable scientist from nearby is commemorated.

There is some very fine stained glass in the cathedral: some early work by Morris and Co, in the easternmost part of the building, more Morris windows in the west wall and some good Shrigley and Hunt glass in the north wall. A recent claim to fame by Bradford is that it was the first cathedral to use solar panels to generate electrical power. In the south transept there are some fine examples of the stained glass work of Charles Eamer Kempe (1837–1907).

Viewed from the north east.

DURHAM CATHEDRAL

The view of Durham when approaching by train is unforgettable. A meander in the River Wear causes a stark outcrop of rock almost to form an island. This island is crowned both by the Norman castle and also by the magnificent strength and nobility of the cathedral. The origins of this great church (a World Heritage Site) lie further back still, in the gentleness of St Cuthbert's mission to the villages and farmsteads within the forests and wild moors of Northumbria. When Cuthbert died in 687 he was buried first on the 'Holy Island' of Lindisfarne. Three hundred years later, following waves of Danish invasions which necessitated the peripatetic movement of the saint's relics throughout Northumbria and the Scottish borders, Cuthbert's remains were reburied in this safe place where Durham Cathedral now stands. Thus began the monastic life of Durham, which was later founded as a Benedictine community. Cuthbert's shrine remains the most sacred place in this stunning building.

Above: Viewed from the River Wear.

Building began in 1093, when Durham was given palatine status by William the Conqueror, during the episcopate of William of St Carilef; the cathedral – built for a prince-bishop who held temporal powers delegated by the monarch – contains undoubtedly the most consistent Romanesque architecture on this scale of any church in England. The main structure of the building took only 42 years to construct, though building continued throughout the twelfth century when the chapter house and Galilee Chapel were added. This western aisled chapel is the second most holy place in this remarkable building, for here is buried the Venerable Bede, who was the first to chronicle the history of the English people in his *Ecclesiastical History of the English People*. Bede drew together the complex threads which combined to form the story of the Roman and the Celtic missions to England; the cathedral's own history is rooted in this rich confluence of tradition.

The cathedral is approached from Palace Green, and entered through the north door, with its splendid twelfth-century Sanctuary Knocker (now a facsimile – the original is in the cathedral museum). The sheer strength and proportion of the building becomes immediately apparent when standing in the nave.

The alternating composite and circular columns with their twisting 'barley sugar' decoration lead the eye up into the choir, and then beyond through the Neville Screen (1380) to the shrine of St Cuthbert, and eventually to the Chapel of the Nine Altars, which forms the easternmost part of the cathedral.

The nave, transepts and choir speak in essence of a consistent use of Romanesque architectural language. The forms are sophisticated, with deeply recessed clerestory windows, bold decoration of the columns, and the earliest rib-vaulting in Europe. The four crossing arches each reach upward to 20 metres (68 feet) in height. The cloister and monastic buildings (including the vast Deanery) also owe their earliest form to the talent of Norman masons.

The story of the cathedral, however, does not end with the Norman builders. Bishop Richard le Poore, in the period 1233–44, replaced a decaying Romanesque apse with a fine Gothic conclusion to the cathedral in the Chapel of the Nine Altars. Bishop Hatfield's tomb of 1333 forms the base of the loftiest episcopal throne in Christendom, later embellished with a seventeenth-century staircase and gallery. St Cuthbert's medieval shrine was lost at the Reformation; now a stone slab is crowned with a colourful tester by Sir Ninian Comper. The medieval screen between choir and nave was sadly removed in the mid-nineteenth century during a period of enthusiasm for openness. It was, however, replaced in 1876 by Sir George Gilbert Scott's marble screen, which acts as a point of transition in one's journey towards the high altar and the shrine.

The outside of the cathedral is given strength and proportion by both the massing of the Romanesque western towers which dominate the bluff overhanging the River Wear, and also by the stately and gently tapering nobility of Bishop Lawrence Booth's central tower; this was completed between 1465 and 1490. Within the building there are other unexpected features. The sixteenth-century clock in the south transept, remodelled in the twentieth century, breathes a somewhat exotic presence in a building which elsewhere speaks of a refined austerity.

Since the Reformation, the monastic buildings have been used variously. The monks' dormitory houses the university's theological library and some 'pre-conquest' stones. The refectory and dormitory now house the cathedral library. The Great Kitchen and the Monks' Dormitory have been refurbished and transformed into the *Open Treasure* exhibition unfolding the history of the building over the past 1,000 years.

The Gilbert Scott screen.

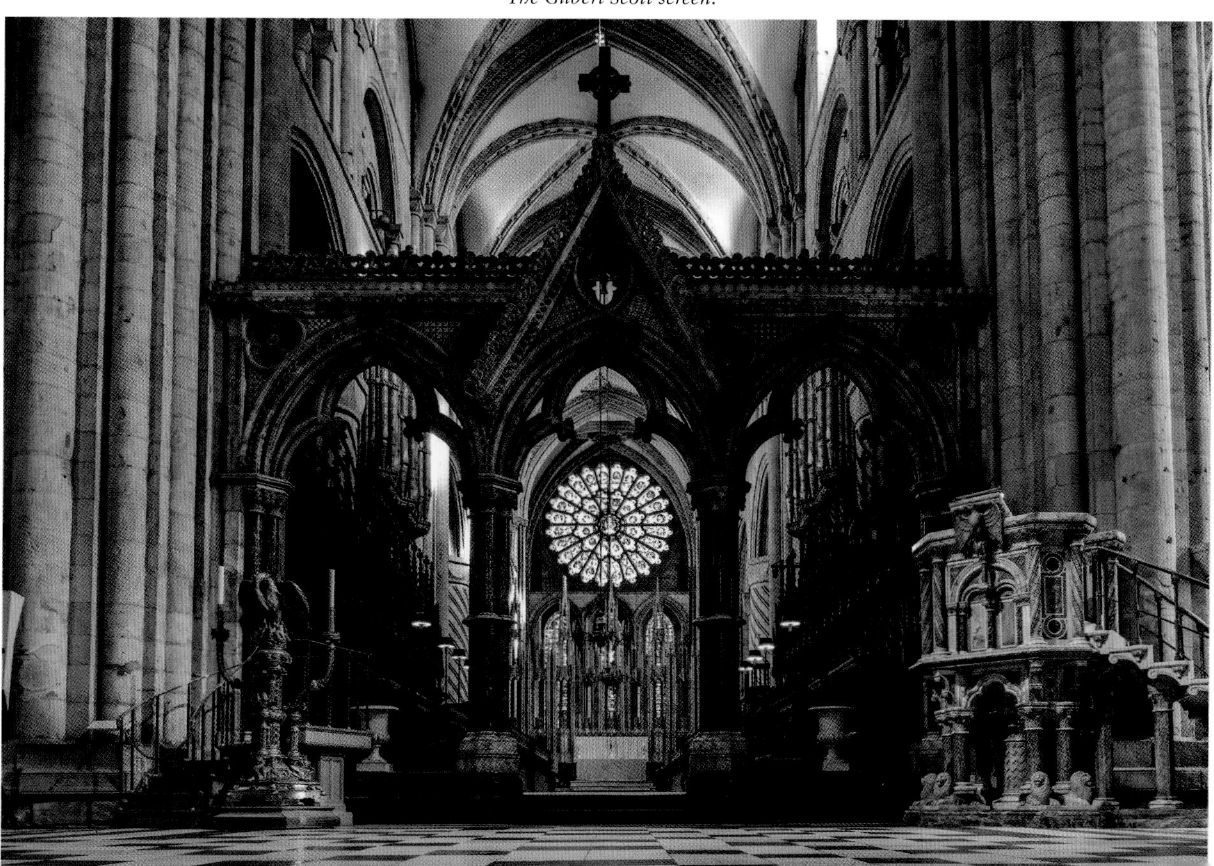

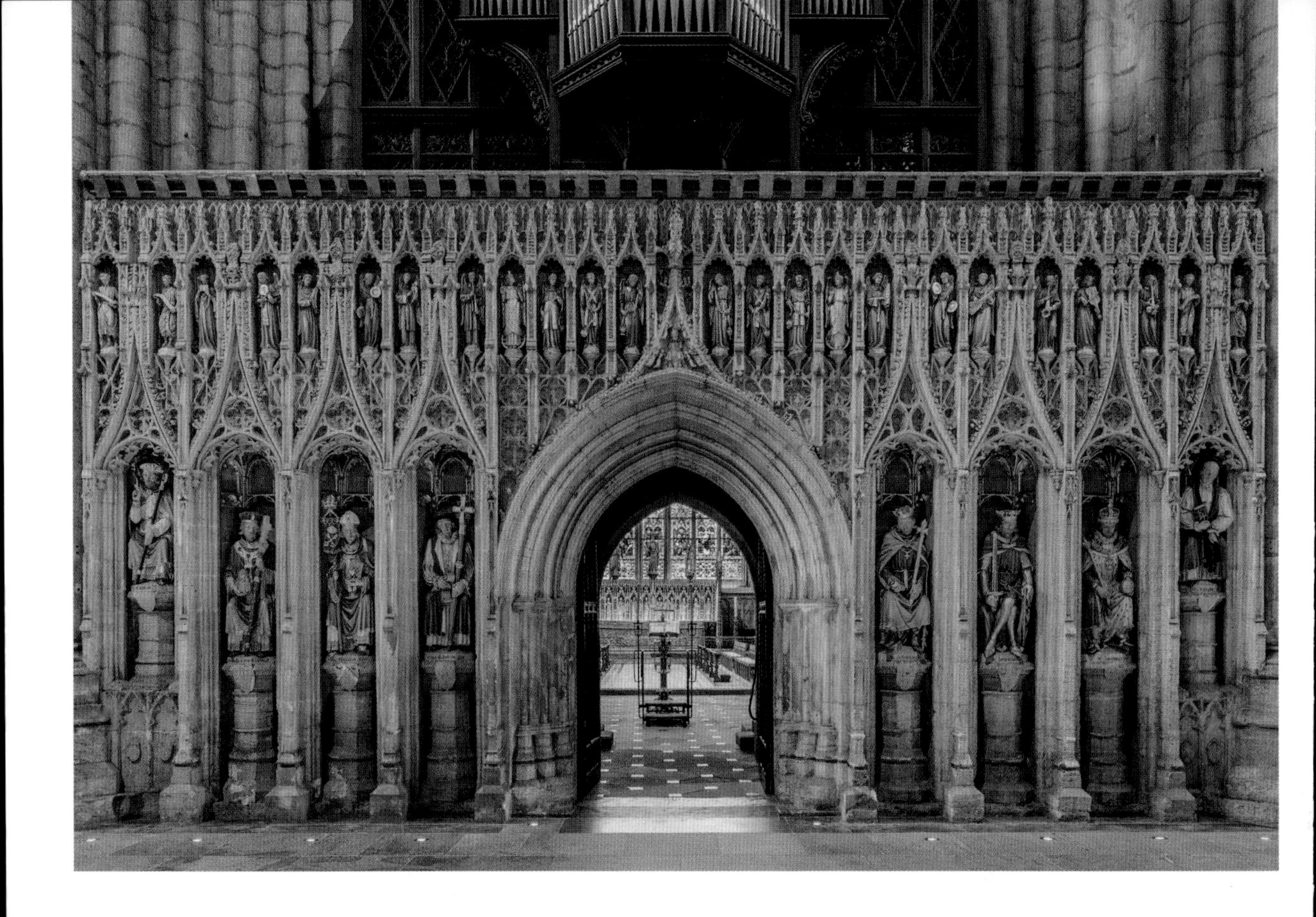

RIPON CATHEDRAL

Ripon Cathedral can rightfully claim to have the oldest fabric of any English cathedral, with the tiny crypt beneath the crossing dating back to 672 when it formed part of Wilfrid's church. Wilfrid, one of the most vigorous of the earlier missionaries to England, was a Northumbrian who embraced the Roman pattern of monastic life. Having travelled to Rome, he brought to Ripon the ancient basilican pattern of church, with its semi-circular east end. Apart from the crypt, all of Wilfrid's church was destroyed in 950. The second minster, which replaced this, was also destroyed, this time by the Normans who, beginning in 1080, decided to build a more magnificent Romanesque building. The earlier foundation was Benedictine from Wilfrid's influence, but the later re-foundation was a college of Augustinian canons.

Approaching the cathedral from the west, one first encounters the splendid Early English west front with its two rows of five lancet windows. This dates from 1220, as does the chapter house. The broad, aisled nave is Perpendicular in style; in 1450 the central tower collapsed causing significant damage to the minster – the present tower and nave date from around 1485, when the rebuilding began. King Edward VI dissolved the college of canons in 1547 before the rebuilding was finished; tell-tale signs of this are clear at the crossing where a Perpendicular pier links to an earlier Romanesque arch. The fine pulpitum screen comes from this period of reconstruction; the earliest of the choir stalls and misericords date from 1494.

The architecture from the crossing into the quire is in the Transitional style, commissioned by Archbishop Roger de Pont L'Evêque. This period of reconstruction gave the minster its present plan. Further through the quire and to the south are the only remains of the Romanesque building of 1080, in the undercroft beneath the chapter house, now the Chapel of the Resurrection. Among interesting furnishings in the cathedral are a Tudor font, an Art Nouveau marble pulpit (1913) and a very fine eastern reredos of 1922, by Sir Ninian Comper, given as a memorial to the dead of the Great War. More recently three bronzes were commissioned by Harold Gosney. Ripon Cathedral is now one of the three cathedrals of the Diocese of Leeds, alongside Bradford and Wakefield.

Above: The choir screen.

YORK MINSTER

Whether one approaches by rail or by road, the massive presence of the minster dominates the plain of York. The dominance of the city as a regional centre can be traced back as far as the fourth century (306) when Constantine was proclaimed emperor at York, and there was a Christian community in the city.

Paulinus' baptising of King Edwin, in 627, led to the building of this first church. Paulinus, the first bishop of York, was followed by Chad in 664 and Wilfrid in 669. York and its minster thus assumed great significance in England from the earliest Christian centuries onwards, contributing one man, Alcuin of York, to European history as organiser of education throughout Charlemagne's empire.

In 1075 Archbishop Thomas began to build a Romanesque church of sufficient size to fit the dignity of the city of York. Although it was called a minster (the Saxon word for monastery) it was always served by secular clergy and was never the home of a religious community. Under three later bishops – Thurstan, William Fitzherbert and Roger de Pont L'Evêque – the Romanesque building was completed. William Fitzherbert, bishop from 1145–47 and then 1153–54, was a Norman nobleman who found himself at the centre of controversy between Church and king, which led to his ten-year deposition. In 1227 he was canonised and became the centre of the modest cult of St William of York. Refashioned fragments of the Romanesque building are still visible in the crypt, near to his shrine. Even this great Romanesque church was to prove inadequate to the dignity of York, and it was in the time of Walter de Gray, archbishop from 1215 to 1255, and with his active support, that the building of the vast and noble Gothic church that we see today was begun. The north and south transepts were built first in the Early English style, including the incomparable Five Sisters window with its tall even lancets (the tallest in Christendom) and subtle grisaille stained glass. De Gray had set in motion a process of reconstruction which extended over a period of

The west front.

The majestic nave.

250 years; his splendid tomb lies in the south transept.

The next stage of rebuilding, from 1260 to 1290, was the construction of the chapter house with its unique octa-pyramidal roof and flying buttresses – the architecture here is rather more delicate. From 1290 to 1360 the masons were set to work on the construction of the broad, majestic, aisled nave for which York is justly celebrated. The scale set by the nave and transepts would eventually transform York into the largest cathedral built in England during the medieval period. The treatment of the clerestory and triforium as part of one unfolding pattern is an innovative feature of the nave. The west front includes three large porticoes and the great west window, one of the chief glories of the minster. The presence of Parliament at York during the Scottish wars in the reigns of Edward I, Edward II and Edward III mean that both glass and statuary in the nave include the shields of the nobility of that time.

The rebuilding of the eastern arm of the minster was begun in the time of Archbishop Thoresby in 1361; this led to the final demise of the Romanesque building during the 1390s. This eastern work began with the Lady Chapel, built in sober Perpendicular with a magnificent great east window; the double tracery here covers an area the size of a tennis court and encloses the largest expanse of medieval painted glass anywhere in the world. Another triumphant feature of this part of the minster is the soaring eastern transept, with its windows running through to the full height of the choir roof. The central tower (which was intended to be completed with a further stage) was built between 1420 and 1430, and by 1465 the west front had been crowned with its two towers.

In 1967 the entire structure was found to be precarious, and urgent action was taken to secure the foundations. Huge concrete supports were created, standing next to the remains of the Roman military quarters, under the central tower. Then, in 1984, fire destroyed the roof of the south transept. Sensitively restored, the timber roof has six bosses designed by children in a competition organised by the BBC. The entire east end, of both stone and glass, has undergone a dramatic feat of conservation. The vast east window is now completely restored. The undercroft exhibition has also been significantly enhanced.

ST ANNE'S CATHEDRAL, LEEDS

St Anne's Church in Cookridge Street, which had been built in 1838, was restyled as a cathedral when the Roman Catholic Diocese of Leeds was founded in 1878. It remained so until the land was compulsorily purchased for road widening and the adjacent site was provided on which a new cathedral would be built.

St Anne's has the interesting distinction of being the only cathedral in Britain in the Arts and Crafts style; it was completed just after the turn of the century, from 1901 to 1904. Designed by John Henry Eastwood, who was Leeds born but London based, it is constructed of Weldon and Ketton stone, and is a noble building of its period, built on a cramped and difficult site. It comprises an aisled nave and chancel all set under one roof space and with no complete transepts on account of the limited site available. The south front is impressive with a gable and gothic turrets. There is a north tower rising directly from the street and a modest octagonal chapter house.

The interior is impressive but not overbearing. The arcades have elements of both gentle Gothic and Art Nouveau featured in the piers and soffits. The reordering of 2005–6 has added further grace and beauty to the interior, especially in the sweeping curve of the steps leading into the chancel-sanctuary. The three-bay Lady Chapel on the south side is of Art Nouveau 'simplified' Gothic, and includes an outstanding reredos by A.W.N. Pugin from the old St Anne's church. The east window is by Eastwood and includes his sun-ray motif.

The aisled nave.

BLACKBURN CATHEDRAL

Set in the midst of post-industrial Blackburn, the cathedral is the jewel in the crown of a burgeoning 'Cathedral Quarter'. The kernel of the building was built by John Palmer in 1820–26. William Temple, while Bishop of Manchester, split his diocese and created a new diocese for the rest of Lancashire. In 1926, St Mary's parish church became the cathedral.

Soon after, William Adam Forsyth was commissioned to extend the church. Work began in 1938 but was halted in 1941 by World War Two, and in 1951 construction was resumed but to a reduced version of Forsyth's original vision. In 1962, Laurence King took up the mantle and worked with the artist John Hayward to complete the cathedral; Hayward was responsible for much of the interior design, artwork and furnishings. The cathedral was finally consecrated in 1977. King's central lantern was rebuilt of natural stone instead of concrete in 1998, following serious corrosion of the structure.

Hayward's corona lifts one's eyes heavenwards, and his *Christ the Worker* at the west end is an equally inspiring piece. Hayward designed the choir furniture, the cathedra and clergy stalls as well as the altar. His dazzling Tree of Life window in the south transept reuses nineteenth-century glass in a powerful abstract design. The nearby font is also by Hayward.

The Laurence King lantern tower.

WAKEFIELD CATHEDRAL

Before its transformation into a cathedral with the foundation of the diocese of Wakefield in 1888, All Saints' was one of the great parish churches of England. Its roots can be traced to Saxon times with the survival of a shaft of a Saxon preaching cross, making Wakefield a more ancient city than nearby Leeds. Work began on the Norman church *c.* 1100, the only surviving element of which is the outside wall of the south transept, near to the Lady Chapel entrance. In the twelfth century an extension was built on the north side, the only clear evidence of this being in the north arcading. The thirteenth century saw further rebuilding of the Norman church, this time on the south side.

The fourteenth century, however, saw the emergence of the triumphant building which we see today. The north and south aisles were widened, and the new church was consecrated in 1329. The tower and spire were not begun until 1420; at 75 metres (247 feet), it is the highest spire in Yorkshire. The chancel and its aisles were under construction in 1458, and probably completed in 1475; the nave clerestory is also from this same period. The chancel's fine misericords include a juggler with his head between his legs, a pelican and a Tudor rose. The font was given in 1661 to mark the Restoration of King Charles II.

The present clarity of the architecture, and its stability, result from the restoration of 1858–74 by Sir George Gilbert Scott. With its new status as a cathedral came the extension to the east, based on draft plans drawn up by John Loughborough Pearson, and completed by his son, Frank. The Pearson extension includes a grand monument to the first bishop, William Walsham How, writer of the hymn 'For all the Saints'. To the east is the retro-quire with St Mark's chapel; there is some fine lierne vaulting.

The screen and rood form a key focus. The screen is an excellent piece of Jacobean work dating from 1635, and the magnificent rood is by Sir Ninian Comper, completed in 1950. The Treacy Memorial Hall to the north is by Peter Marshall and was completed in 1982. From 2012 onwards the cathedral was transformed by clearing the pews from the nave and reordering the choir and crypt, giving an entirely new sense of space. The Saxon Cross was installed outside the west end of the cathedral in 2016. It was designed and cut by Celia Kilner who also designed the labyrinth and lettering around the font in the nave.

The nave looking west.

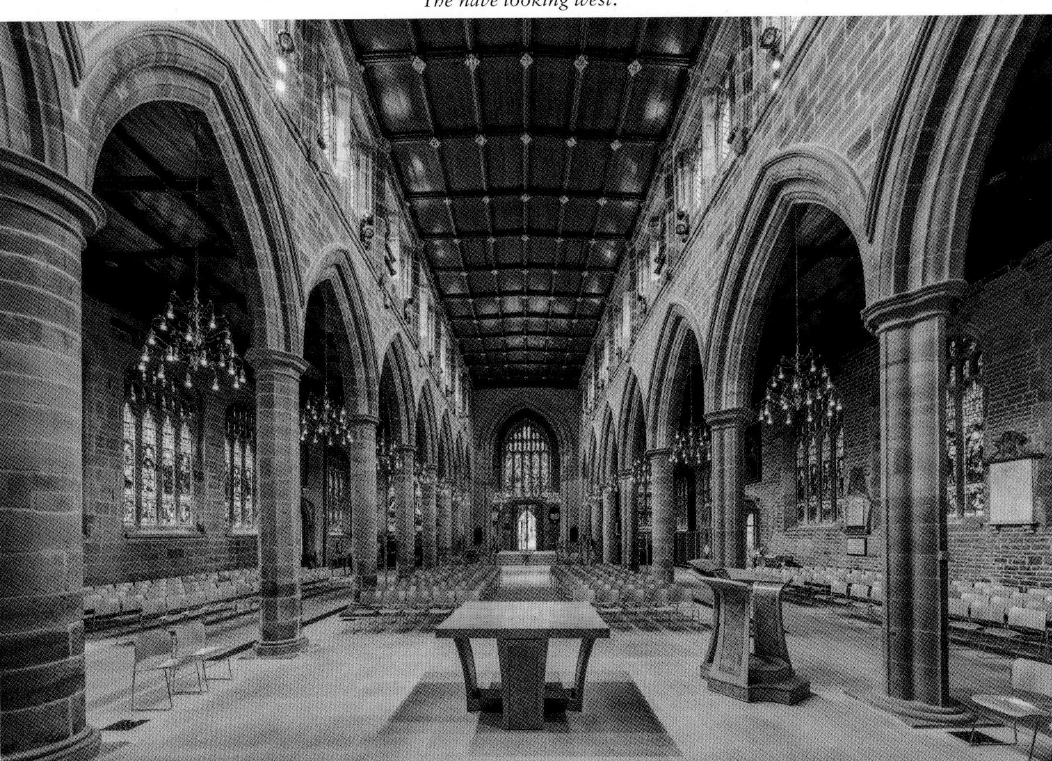

MANCHESTER CATHEDRAL

Set in the heart of a northern industrial city, it is easy to underestimate the historic roots of Manchester Cathedral. The attractive grouping of buildings comprising the cathedral and Chethams Hospital School and Library are the direct descendants of the collegiate church established by King Henry V in 1421. The roots probably extend still further back, for, in 1871, when the greater part of the south porch was dismantled, an unusual carved stone was discovered, since known as 'The Angel Stone'. This probably came from the tympanum over the south door of the Saxon church of St Mary; the theme of the carving is the Annunciation.

The origins of the present church are effectively from the early fifteenth century when it gained collegiate status. The quire and quire aisles date from this early period and were built by John Huntington, the first warden of the college and rector of the church. From 1465 to 1481 the nave was rebuilt and Huntington's chapter house was completed around 1485. Within the nave, the double aisles were formed from earlier chantry chapels. The church became a cathedral with the establishment of Manchester diocese in 1847. The quire chantries survived; these include the Jesus Chapel (1516) and the Regimental Chapel, founded as the Chantry of St John the Baptist in the early sixteenth century.

One of the most splendid features of the medieval fabric is the woodwork, with some excellent misericords, quire stall canopies and bench ends. The pulpitum screen is very fine and has been enhanced by the completion of the new organ with its case by Stephen Raw. Although the cathedral is substantially late medieval, there is some modern work. There were two significant restorations in the nineteenth century – the second helped redress some of the harm done in the earlier restoration and gave a new dignity to the building. The modern Lady Chapel replaces that destroyed by aerial bombing in 1940. There is a modern stone carving of the Christ Child by Eric Gill, five particularly fine stained-glass windows by Anthony Hollaway, and the stunning Fire Window in the Regimental Chapel.

Above: The early fifteenth-century choir.

LIVERPOOL CATHEDRAL

Sir Giles Gilbert Scott's Cathedral Church of Christ, in its magnificent position, atop St James' Mount in Liverpool, is undoubtedly the triumph of twentieth-century Gothic. The story of its construction over the period from 1904–78 mirrors the building of the great medieval cathedrals. Part of the achievement is the sheer nobility and scale of the building. Alongside this, however, Scott never lost sight of a concern for detail and decoration. The cathedral is dominated by the majestic Vestey tower, either side of which are the twin eastern and western transepts which enfold, on the north and south sides, the Welsford and Rankin porches.

To enter the cathedral from the west is to be almost overwhelmed with the impression of space, looking through the noble span of the nave bridge into the building's core which allows enormous flexibility for worship. The arches enclosing it, which rise to 32 metres (107 feet) at their apexes, are the largest Gothic arches ever built. The space is beautifully enclosed by the transepts and porches. The transepts are variously conceived: one is the War Memorial Chapel, a second is now the visitor centre crowned by Keith Scott's sail-like aerial sculpture *The Spirit of Liverpool*, and a third contains the memorial to the Earl of Derby whose support was so important in the early building of the cathedral. The fourth (the south-western) transept is the baptistry with its fine font of buff-coloured French marble surmounted by a soaring oak baldachino.

To the east is the high altar with its intricately gilded reredos, including scenes of the Passion, Crucifixion and Last Supper. In the south choir aisle are the entrances to the Lady Chapel and its gallery. This was the first part of the cathedral to be completed (1910). Its more ornate style focuses on the influence of G.F. Bodley who was appointed to work with the young Giles Gilbert Scott when construction began. A further glory of the building is the glass, crowned by Carl Edwards' splendid meditation on the Benedicite in the great west window.

Contemporary artistic commissions include paintings by Adrian Wizniewski and Christopher Le Brun, Elisabeth Frink's sculpture *Welcoming Christ* over the west door, and *Calvary 1998* by Craigie Aitchison.

Above: The 100-metre (330-foot) tower.

High altar, reredos and great east window.

LIVERPOOL METROPOLITAN CATHEDRAL

In the 1930s Sir Edwin Lutyens designed a monumental church to be built on a new site astride the same hill as Scott's Anglican cathedral. Only the crypt, however, with its notable six-ton circular 'rolling gate', was completed before the outbreak of war in 1939. Twenty years later Frederick Gibberd was appointed as architect for the cathedral and he used the crypt as a basic platform for his design. At the other end of Hope Street from Scott's great church, Liverpool Metropolitan Cathedral makes an eloquent ecumenical statement in this city of divided religious traditions. Crowning the city of Liverpool, it stands in complementary contrast to Scott's neo-Gothic building, and together they produce a dramatic skyline. The cathedral's circular plan was revolutionary at the time. The lantern crowning the cathedral is a stunning sight both in daylight and at night, when it acts as a beacon on the city's skyline. The glass is by John Piper and Patrick Reyntiens, who had worked together earlier on the baptistry window in the cathedral at Coventry. More recently, the nave floor has been replaced and a magnificent new organ screen has been completed at the entrance to the choir.

Left: Viewed from the west.

SHEFFIELD CATHEDRAL

When the Diocese of Sheffield was founded in 1914, the parish church of St Peter and St Paul became the new cathedral. It has had a chequered history. By the end of the eighteenth century, the church was increasingly ruinous. In 1878–1880 there was a major restoration by Flockton and Gibbs under the tutelage of Sir Gilbert Scott. North and south transepts were added.

In the twentieth century, the complexity of the building increased, however, when Sir Charles Nicholson produced a radical plan to change the orientation of the church entirely to a north–south axis. Work began in 1937, but war intervened and once again shortage of funds meant that an incomplete building was dedicated.

Ultimately, Arthur Bailey returned the building to its original orientation, completing the building with a new western crossing in the nave. The building was consecrated in 1966. The new angled Gateway entrance of 2015 offers an intriguing way into the building. Amber Hiscott's rebuilt western lantern pours plentiful light into the church. Nicholson's intended 'east end' forms the Chapel of the Holy Spirit with rich furnishing by Ninian Comper. One of the jewels of the building is the late Gothic Shrewsbury Chapel, built by the Earls of Shrewsbury including remarkable Tudor tombs.

Above: The new Gateway entrance was added in 2015.
Right: Coventry Cathedral.

THE MIDLANDS

The region described as the Midlands might well begin with Lichfield, where the Christian church was established particularly early, by St Chad who brought the Celtic tradition with him. In the late eighth century, for a short period, Lichfield achieved metropolitan status, with an archbishop. The Norman hegemony in England can be traced in the splendid nave at Southwell Minster and also in the outstanding Romanesque frieze in the west front at Lincoln.

Lincoln, one of the most magnificent ecclesiastical buildings of England, is a triumph of medieval Gothic. Birmingham Cathedral is a fine example of eighteenth-century Classical architecture. Coventry Cathedral can boast works by a number of the great contemporary artists of the twentieth century. Leicester Cathedral brings with it one of the most dramatic periods of English and is the last resting place of King Richard III.

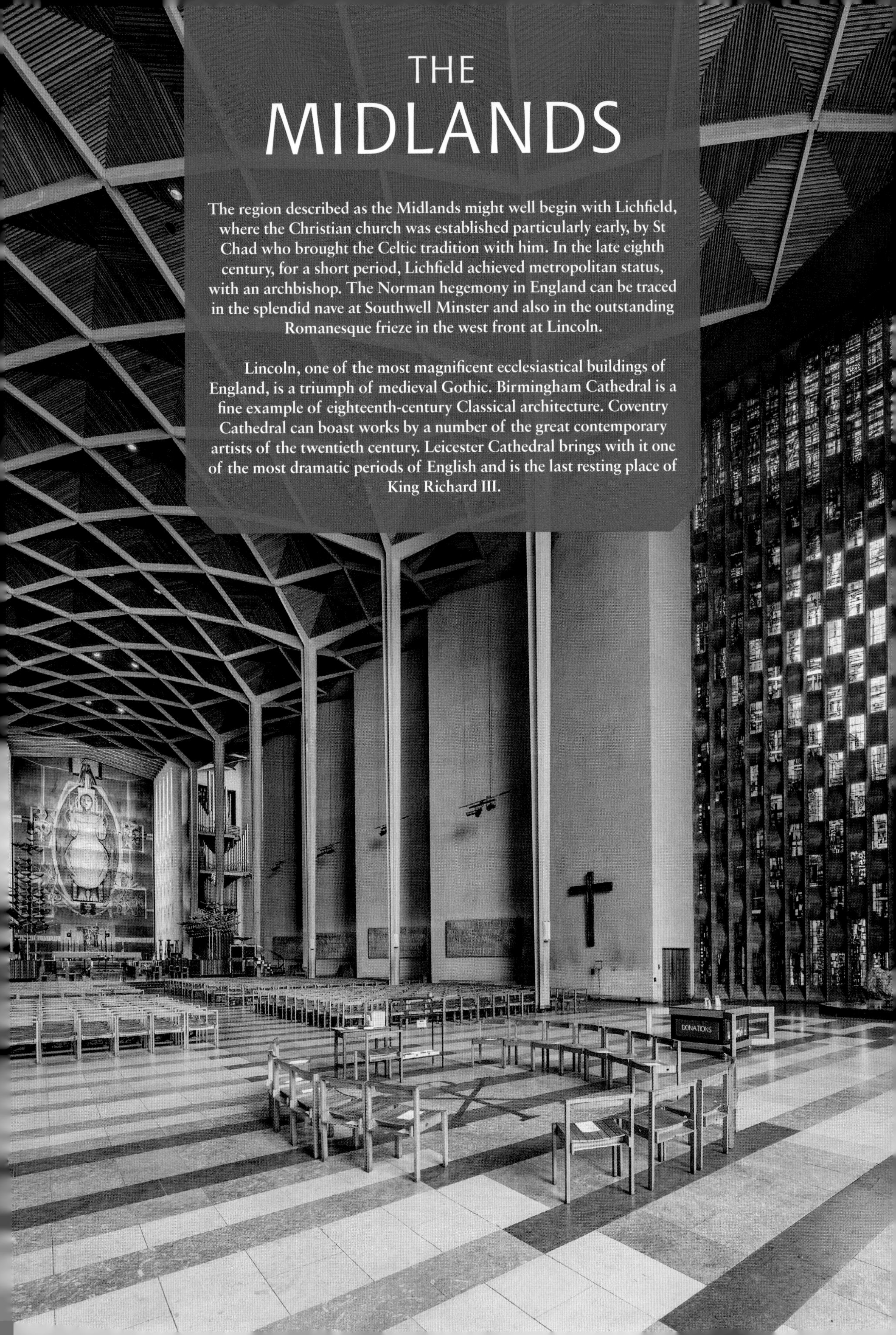

CHESTER CATHEDRAL

The origins of Chester date back to *c.* AD 79 when the Romans built a fortress on the River Dee. In the tenth century the remains of St Werburgh, a seventh-century Mercian saint, were brought to Chester to protect them from the Danes; Werburgh had been a nun and a great exemplar of the Christian life. Her relics were placed in a Saxon minster, which was enlarged to house her shrine. After the Norman Conquest, the second Earl of Chester re-founded the church as a Benedictine abbey. St Anselm, Abbot of Bec in Normandy and later Archbishop of Canterbury, brought monks in 1092 to establish the abbey. After the Dissolution of the Monasteries in 1541 King Henry VIII handed the monastery over to become the cathedral of the new diocese of Chester.

The Romanesque building took 150 years to build; only fragments of the Norman work survive, notably in the baptistry and the north transept. By the end of this period of rebuilding, Transitional pointed arches began to emerge in the monastic buildings around the cloister.

The change of style prompted the second rebuilding of the abbey church itself in Gothic style, beginning with the Early English Lady Chapel of around 1275. The nave dates from the late fifteenth century. The choir is Early English of around 1200; the splendid stalls and misericords were probably carved in about 1380.

St Werburgh's Chapel is in the north choir aisle, while her shrine survives in the nearby Lady Chapel. The tower over the crossing is late medieval, but the corner turrets were added during the nineteenth-century restoration by Sir George Gilbert Scott. The large south transept is aisled and contains a series of chapels. There is a fine reredos in the chapel of St Oswald by C.E. Kempe. Much of the monastic complex survives; the cloisters were largely rebuilt between 1525 and 1537. The unusual detached bell tower of 1975 is by George Pace.

The magnificent Creation window in the refectory was designed by Rosalind Grimshaw and installed in 2001. A new Song School designed by Andrew Arrol was built over the cloisters in 2005.

The cloister.

DERBY CATHEDRAL

The classical nave.

Derby Cathedral's fine early sixteenth-century Perpendicular tower is deceptive, for it speaks neither of the antiquity of the site nor the style of most of the present building. The earliest church was a Saxon foundation established by King Edmund *c.* 943 as a royal collegiate church, with a dean and six prebendaries. In the fourteenth century this church was replaced, but in 1723 all but the tower was demolished, and James Gibbs (the architect of St Martin-in-the-Fields in London and the Radcliffe Camera in Oxford) built the beautiful restrained Classical building which we see today, with its magnificent wrought iron screen. The cathedral has a similar balance and feel to St Martin-in-the-Fields. The nave and aisles are separated by Tuscan columns on tall pedestals to allow for box pews.

The foundation of Derby diocese in 1927 made All Saints the cathedral, and in 1965 Sebastian Comper extended the building following designs modified from those of his father, Sir Ninian Comper. Sebastian Comper's addition reflects the architecture of James Gibbs and effectively adds the impressive retrochoir with a Chapter Room and Song School beneath. The choir stalls and pulpit by Temple Moore and the windows by Ceri Richards are fine additions. Among the many monuments in the cathedral, which originate from the medieval church, is the sumptuous tomb of Bess of Hardwick, one of the richest women in Tudor England by the time of her death in 1608.

SOUTHWELL MINSTER

Set in the smallest 'cathedral town' in England, Southwell Cathedral's two western spires are reminiscent of Rheinland architecture. In 1884 the minster became the cathedral of the new diocese. Remains of the palace of the archbishops of York can be seen to the south of the cathedral.

Entering at the west end, one encounters the awesome strength of the nave, dominated by the drum-like pillars. Further down the nave are the noble Romanesque arches of the crossing, carved with rope mouldings. The two transepts are also Romanesque. The splendid Decorated pulpitum of *c.* 1340, with its vaulted vestibule and canopied stalls, leads into the quire, which is built in a light Early English style. From the north choir aisle a passage leads to the magnificent late thirteenth-century chapter house; built in the Decorated style and famous for its leaf carvings, it is the only octagonal chapter house in England.

The new Great West Window was dedicated on 7 July 1996. Conceived by Martin Stancliffe, it was designed and painted by Patrick Reyntiens; the window brings a great gathering of angels to the minster. Significant new artwork has been commissioned for the minster including Nicholas Mynheer's War Memorial Window and Plaque.

Right: The western 'pepperpot' towers.

LINCOLN CATHEDRAL

There is perhaps no other cathedral in England in such a breathtaking position as Lincoln. Enthroned high on a limestone cliff that runs north to south, it stands like a great ocean liner at anchor. Presumably it was constructed to dominate the vast diocese over which its bishop ruled. Like Norwich, Lincoln is an example of a cathedral being moved by the Norman conquerors to a strategically important centre. Bishop Remigius moved his see city here from Dorchester-on-Thames in 1072, six years after the Norman Conquest. The 11th-century west front has been preserved and framed by the later Gothic work. Incomparable are the frieze panels of the flood and other biblical scenes; the whole frieze is being conserved and copies are being made to replace the most damaged original panels.

An earth tremor caused damage to the Romanesque cathedral in 1185. It was St Hugh of Avalon, a Carthusian monk and a great medieval bishop, who rebuilt the cathedral, starting from the east. He kept the Norman towers and the great facade dating from Bishop Remigius' time as the sumptuous frame for the west door, to retain what John Ruskin described as one of the artistic wonders of Europe. Entering Lincoln through the great west door is in itself an enthralling experience. As the cavernous, yet majestic, interior opens up, the sheer scale on which the cathedral is built becomes apparent. The nave is not over-high, but it is both wide and long, with a mixture of Purbeck marble and limestone in its strong Gothic piers; the vaulting is plain but in scale with the rest of the nave, which has relatively modest triforium and clerestory levels.

The interior of the west front is distinguished by the lattice pattern in the stonework, said to be a trademark of one of the other great medieval builders of Lincoln, Bishop Robert Grosseteste.

The impressive size of the building can be appreciated from the crossing. The vaulting of the tower rises to 38 metres (125 feet) and the two transepts are in proportion to the nave. At the end of the south transept is the Bishop's Eye, a fine circular window which looks out over the ruins of

Above: The impressive west front.

the medieval bishop's palace. Directly opposite, lighting the north transept, is another circular window, the Dean's Eye, overlooking the site of the earlier Deanery. Each transept has three chapels on its eastern side, and at the end of the south transept is a strong but sensitive sculpture of Edward King, the saintly bishop of Lincoln during the latter part of the nineteenth and beginning of the twentieth century.

Beyond the elaborate fourteenth-century screen lies St Hugh's Choir, named in honour of its builder. The vaulting here is unusual with the asymmetry of the ribs. Some fine medieval ironwork opens out into the north-eastern and south-eastern transepts. The north-eastern transept leads into the cloister. Here is a sure sign that Lincoln was not a monastic cathedral – monastic cloisters were built to the south to catch the sun. The northern walk of the cloister is enclosed by a noble and restrained library by Sir Christopher Wren. To the east stands the fine polygonal Gothic chapter house.

At the eastern end of the cathedral is the Angel Choir, the apotheosis of English Decorated Gothic, constructed as a means of housing the much-visited head shrine of St Hugh. In front of the shrine the paving is worn away through the constant kneeling of devout pilgrims. The Angel Choir is a daring conclusion to this majestic building with its trefoils, clustered pillars and angels reaching out from the higher levels. On the north arcade, facing south, is the famous Lincoln imp, one of 16 grotesques.

With its three vast towers, Lincoln cathedral dominates the city. The central tower, completed in the early fourteenth century, reaches a height of 80 metres (262 feet). All three towers were surmounted by spires until the sixteenth century, with the central spire rising to a height of 160 metres (524 feet). It was said to have been visible from East Anglia. The cathedral still crowns the county of Lincolnshire as a living and majestic piece of English Gothic. The 'Lincoln Cathedral Connected' project will provide new hospitality and interpretation facilities on the north side of the cathedral.

The pulpitum screen.

LICHFIELD CATHEDRAL

The origins of Lichfield Cathedral lie in the building of a church in 700 as a shrine for St Chad, who was taught by St Aidan at Lindisfarne, and was bishop from 668 to 672. In 1140 the Saxon church was replaced by Bishop Clinton's Romanesque building. This building had probably been started in 1085 and originally, in following the Norman pattern, it had an apsidal end to the choir. A larger church was begun in 1195, leading eventually to the completion of the present building in 1340. The choir, choir aisles, presbytery and central tower were completed in Norman Transitional and Early English styles. The north and south transepts followed in 1220 and 1240 respectively; again the style is Early English and there is some elegant blind arcading. Unusually, the chapter house of 1249 has two storeys, with the attractive central column passing through both levels. The vestibule to the chapter house includes a fascinating feature, a place where on Maundy Thursday the foot-washing took place. There are 13 seats where the poor whose feet were being washed would have sat. The greatest treasure of the library is St Chad's gospels, dating from around 735.

In 1285 the present nave was completed in a Transitional style between Early English and Decorated. From the west end there is a splendid view of the entire length of the cathedral, since all the roof levels through to the Lady Chapel are at the same height. The west front with its twin spires was not finished until 1327. The Lady Chapel of 1330–40, with its graceful, lofty windows, was built in the Decorated style. St Chad's shrine was later moved into this chapel. Excavation for a nave altar platform in 2003 suggests that the Shrine of St Chad was originally in the nave. It was moved to the Lady Chapel around the turn of the fourteenth century because of the number of pilgrims. A magnificent mid-Saxon stone carving of the Archangel Gabriel, found during the excavation, may have formed part of the earlier shrine, which disappeared at the Reformation. In 1225 the Chapel of St Chad's Head was added on the south side. The skull of the saint was kept in a casket here.

Looking towards the high altar.

LEICESTER CATHEDRAL

The church, as we now see it, owes most to the nineteenth century, when there was a series of restorations. G.E. Street rebuilt the north aisle and in 1896–98, J.L. Pearson rebuilt the south aisle and added the dignified south porch. More recently, in 1927, when the parish church of St Martin was designated cathedral for the new diocese of Leicester, Sir Charles Nicholson was commissioned to redesign the interior. Following the recent reordering at the time of the reinterment of the King's remains, a new cathedra was commissioned which has received mixed reviews.

The north and south arcades are from the mid-fifteenth century, when the nave was also lengthened by one bay. In the outer south aisle is the furniture of an Archdeacon's court.

The discovery of the remains of King Richard III, beneath a car park just 150 metres south of St Martin's, in 2012, has transformed one of our lesser-known cathedrals into a magnet for visitors from all over Britain and well beyond. After their rediscovery his remains were reinterred in the equivalent position they had occupied in the former Greyfriars friary church when he was buried there in 1485. The new tomb is fashioned out of Swaledale fossil stone. To the north, in St Katharine's Chapel, are Thomas Denny's splendid Redemption Windows, commissioned and dedicated at the same time as the reinterment.

Left: Tomb of King Richard and Nicholson screen.

BIRMINGHAM CATHEDRAL

Birmingham is perhaps the most remarkable example of a city born of the Industrial Revolution. In 1708 an Act of Parliament allowed the new parish of St Philip to be established. St Philip's was architect Thomas Archer's first church and is in the style of a restrained Italian baroque similar to the work of Borromini. The main structure was completed by 1715, and ten years later the western domed tower was added.

The church was built of brick, faced with stone from Archer's own estate. The eastern end concluded with a shallow apse which was extended with a powerful chancel by the architect J.A. Chatwin between 1882 and 1888. His concept was impressive with projecting Corinthian columns and a fine marbled finish. Into this new chancel were placed three windows by Edward Burne-Jones, the Pre-Raphaelite artist, who had been born in nearby Bennet's Hill.

The twentieth-century relief of Bishop Barnes is by sculptor David Wynne. Outside there is a striking statue of Charles Gore, the first Bishop of Birmingham, a celebrated theologian and one of the co-founders of the Community of the Resurrection. In 1980–82, Michael Reardon reordered the interior offering more space and in 1989 built an underground meeting room and Song School.

Right: Chancel with Burne-Jones windows.

COVENTRY CATHEDRAL

To visit Coventry Cathedral is to make a pilgrimage which is both unique and symbolic among all the cathedrals of England. It is profoundly moving to stand in the ruins of the old nave, gazing upon the cross of charred timbers and the cross of nails with the two words, 'Father, Forgive'. The building of the cathedral caught the imagination of people throughout the world. It was seen as a phoenix rising from the ashes, offering itself to a continuing ministry of reconciliation.

The Christian roots of Coventry lie in the foundation of a nunnery by St Osburga. In 1043 Earl Leofric of Mercia and his countess, Lady Godiva, founded the Benedictine priory of St Mary, which became the cathedral of the diocese of Coventry and Lichfield. With the establishment of the new diocese of Coventry in 1918, the fourteenth-century Perpendicular parish church of St Michael became the second cathedral in Coventry's history. Following the destruction of much of the city through aerial bombardment in 1940, only ruins of this building remain.

Almost immediately after the blitz there emerged plans to rebuild, but it was not until 1956 that the foundation stone of Basil Spence's new cathedral was laid. Spence conceived his plan on the assumption that both the ruin and the new building

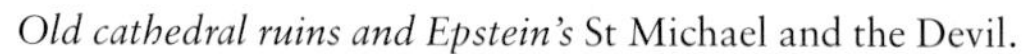

Old cathedral ruins and Epstein's St Michael and the Devil.

Interior with Graham Sutherland tapestry.

formed a unity. John Hutton's splendid western screen of engraved glass reinforces this feeling. The new building, of pink sandstone, is entered on the south side through a vast porch distinguished by the striking sculpture *St Michael and the Devil* by Sir Jacob Epstein.

On entering the nave, the focus is Graham Sutherland's huge tapestry *Christ in Glory*, beneath which lies the Lady Chapel. On turning westward the cleverly slanted nave windows, the work of Lawrence Lee, Keith New and Geoffrey Clarke can be justly admired.

The baptistry window was designed by John Piper and made by Patrick Reyntiens; the Chapel of Christ in Gethsemane has a screen based on a crown of thorns, while the Chapel of Unity is a further symbol of reconciliation – this time between the different churches of the Christian tradition. In 1990 a statue, *Reconciliation* by Josefina de Vasconcellos, was placed in the ruins of the cathedral with an identical casting being placed in the Peace Memorial Park in Hiroshima.

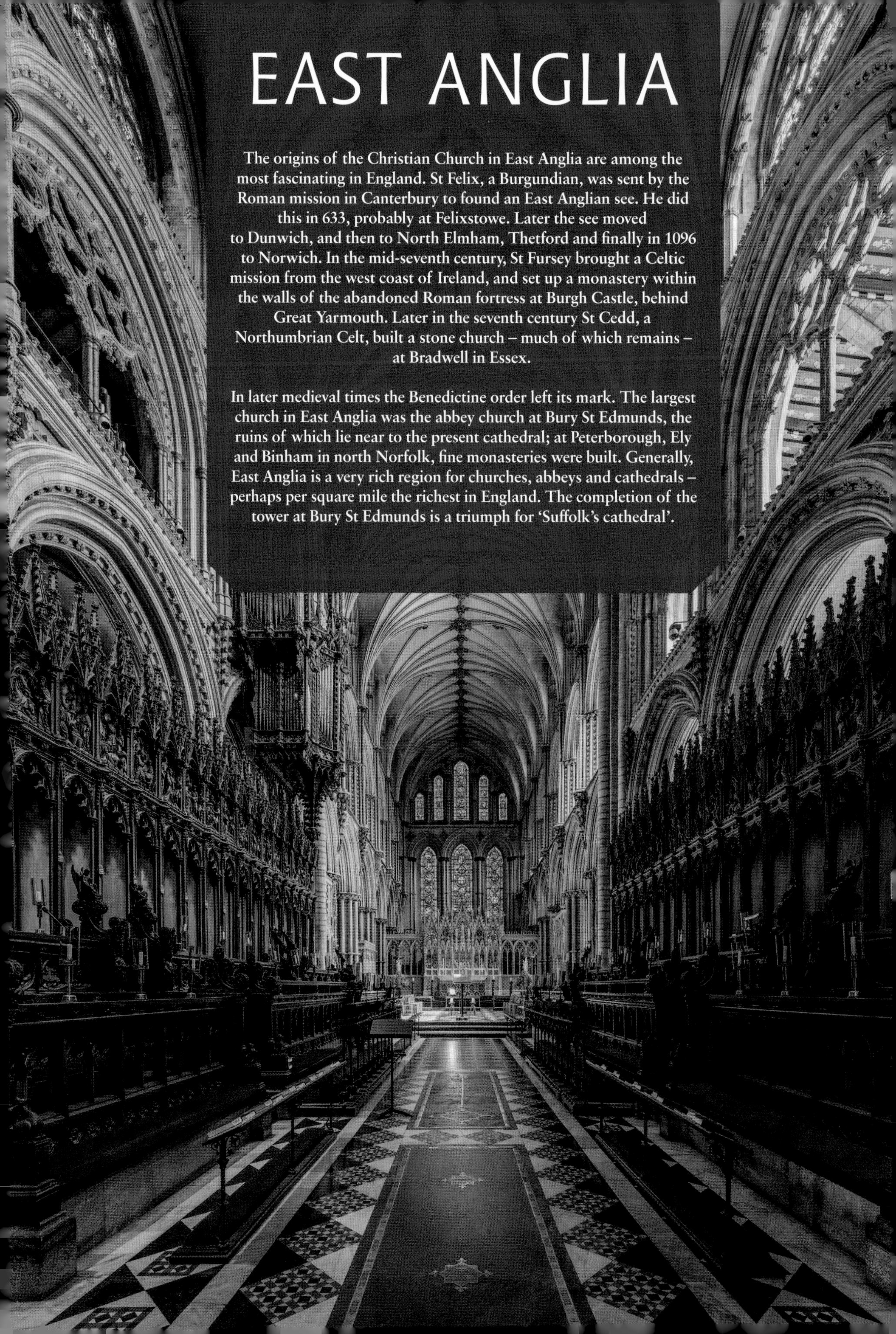

EAST ANGLIA

The origins of the Christian Church in East Anglia are among the most fascinating in England. St Felix, a Burgundian, was sent by the Roman mission in Canterbury to found an East Anglian see. He did this in 633, probably at Felixstowe. Later the see moved to Dunwich, and then to North Elmham, Thetford and finally in 1096 to Norwich. In the mid-seventh century, St Fursey brought a Celtic mission from the west coast of Ireland, and set up a monastery within the walls of the abandoned Roman fortress at Burgh Castle, behind Great Yarmouth. Later in the seventh century St Cedd, a Northumbrian Celt, built a stone church – much of which remains – at Bradwell in Essex.

In later medieval times the Benedictine order left its mark. The largest church in East Anglia was the abbey church at Bury St Edmunds, the ruins of which lie near to the present cathedral; at Peterborough, Ely and Binham in north Norfolk, fine monasteries were built. Generally, East Anglia is a very rich region for churches, abbeys and cathedrals – perhaps per square mile the richest in England. The completion of the tower at Bury St Edmunds is a triumph for 'Suffolk's cathedral'.

NORWICH CATHEDRAL

At 96 metres (315 feet) Norwich's spire is the second highest in England, but it does not dominate its surrounding landscape like Salisbury. This is because Bishop Herbert de Losinga, on moving the see from Thetford to Norwich, chose to place the cathedral close to the heart of the existing town. This put the cathedral and priory on the edge of the marshy flood plain of the River Wensum. Remarkably, the 'footprint' of the monastic demesne established by Herbert in 1096 is almost exactly the same as that marking out the Close and cathedral precincts in the present day. It was in 1096 that construction began of the best preserved Romanesque cathedral in England. The floor plan still retains the apsidal east end, and in the nave the Norman architecture survives throughout the three levels from the floor, up through the triforium to the clerestory.

There is much to be said for beginning a visit to the cathedral by walking up from Pull's Ferry, the water-gate, to the Close. This Gothic arch on the riverbank originally guarded the entrance to a canal which led up to the lower close. On this canal the Caen stone, ferried via Great Yarmouth and the River Yare, made its way to its final destination as the new cathedral took shape. Next to the granary range stands the Prior's House, now the Deanery. This building retains some thirteenth-century work, including the Prior's Hall. Its south front, however, comprises a mixture of styles – Georgian, stepped Flemish gables, and medieval walls. Until the nineteenth century there would have been buildings connecting the Deanery with the cloister and priory

Above: Spire from the cloister.
Opposite: Ely Cathedral.

buildings. The cloister is entered from the north-east, through the old chapter house entrance. It is the largest monastic cloister in England, and, following a fire in 1272, was rebuilt over a period of 150 years. A walk around the cloister offers a graphic history of English tracery.

Entering the cathedral by the monks' door, in the north-west corner of the cloister, the Romanesque nave, crowned by Bishop Lyhart's magnificent lierne vault, is an impressive sight as it stretches away in its record number of 14 bays. Embellishing the nave vault are some of the cathedral's 1,100 roof bosses. Starting from the crossing, these tell the Christian story of creation and redemption. The three easternmost bays of the nave form the choir, which is entered through Lyhart's pulpitum screen, surmounted by Stephen Dykes Bower's noble modern organ case. To the right, beneath the pulpitum, is the Chapel of the Holy Innocents, honouring all those who, through the centuries, have died innocently due to the cruelty of others.

The fifteenth-century misericords are very fine, and continue beyond the choir stalls and over into the crossing. The strength of the Romanesque is nowhere more evident than in the shafts at the crossing, which bear the weight of the tower. Norwich was the tallest Norman cathedral tower and the unique patterning on the exterior probably dates back to the original masons and their work of around 1100. The two transepts also contain good Romanesque work at the higher levels, and particularly the north transept, which includes the Millennium Incarnation window by John Hayward. The south transept was restored at floor level and on its southern façade by Anthony Salvin in the nineteenth century. The presbytery is an uncluttered Romanesque basilican space; the placing of the bishop's throne high up in the eastern apse is unique in northern Europe.

The magnificent clerestory and vaulting is the joint work of two bishops – Bishop Percy in the fourteenth century and Bishop Goldwell in the fifteenth century. The delicacy of Bishop Percy's clerestory window tracery required Bishop Goldwell's masons to use flying buttresses to support the weight of the vaulting. The ambulatory, the almost circular St Luke's and Jesus Chapels, and the reliquary niche beneath the bishop's throne are again unique to Norwich. Now set in this niche is a modern icon of the Resurrection of Christ. In St Luke's Chapel is the Despenser Retable, one of the cathedral's remarkable paintings, dating back to 1381, depicting the Passion and its sequel.

Outside, to the east of the south door, on Life's Green, is the grave of Edith Cavell, a heroine of the First World War. South of the cloister is the award-winning visitor and education centre known as 'The Hostry'. It was designed by Sir Michael Hopkins and completed in 2009, bringing new life into the cloister garth.

Choir and presbytery.

ROMAN CATHOLIC CATHEDRAL OF ST JOHN THE BAPTIST, NORWICH

The Roman Catholic cathedral of St John the Baptist crowns one of the highest points in Norwich, and is a notable landmark within the city. It was built by the 15th Duke of Norfolk who was also responsible for the fine Roman Catholic Cathedral at Arundel, in Sussex. The cathedral, begun in 1882, is the work of Sir George Gilbert Scott Junior and is in the Early English style. With its strong central tower it is conceived on a large scale with an aisled nave of ten bays and an aisled sanctuary. The north aisle of the sanctuary is a chapel dedicated to the Precious Blood, and the south aisle forms a sacrament chapel. The cathedral is cruciform and the triple lancet window in the north transept is said to have been designed by the Duke of Norfolk himself. The first wife of the 15th Duke, in whose memory he gave the money for the cathedral, is remembered in the Chapel of St Joseph. A new connecting and welcoming area has been added at the west end.

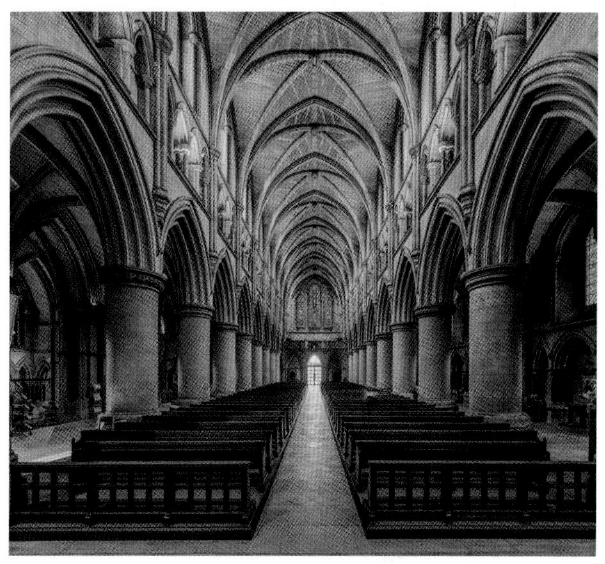

The aisled nave.

BRENTWOOD CATHEDRAL

The earliest part of the present Roman Catholic cathedral at Brentwood dates from 1861, when a parish church was built in neo-Gothic style. In 1989 work began on a building to adjoin the church and was completed two years later to a design by Quinlan Terry. The style is Classical, a mixture of early Italian Renaissance and Wren. The building is effectively a hall-like structure after the fashion of some of the City of London 'preaching boxes'. The Classical motif is carried through with great elegance and the retention of the Gothic Revival work adds interest.

Surmounting the Classical arcading are terracotta roundels. The climax of the building is a lantern, lit with round-headed clear-leaded lights; at the apex of the lantern is a dome and finally a cross. The bishop's chair and the ambo were both made in Pisa, of Nabrassina stone. The cathedral is lit by ornate brass chandeliers, crowning the feeling of elegance and light. The Blessed Sacrament Chapel is part of the remaining 1861 Gothic Revival church.

The nave's brass chandeliers.

PETERBOROUGH CATHEDRAL

The west front of Peterborough Cathedral with its vast Gothic triple portico is unique in Christendom. The roots of the cathedral lie in a monastery founded by Paeda, king of Mercia, in 655. This monastery, established by Northumbrian missionaries, would have followed the Celtic pattern; a survival from the Saxon period is the Hedda Stone in the apse, dating from around 780. In 870 the monastery was pillaged by the Danes, and the community came to an end. Later a new Benedictine community was established, and the larger abbey church was consecrated in 972, in the presence of King Edgar.

The present building was begun in 1118 following a fire two years earlier. By 1140, all of the Norman work east of the crossing was complete; the apse has survived along with arcading. From 1133 to 1178 work went ahead on the crossing, transepts and east end of the nave, all of which have retained their Romanesque purity – apart from the insertion of Gothic arches on the east-west axis, when the Norman tower became unstable around 1335. The present tower is in the Decorated style.

The west end of the nave is the work of Abbot Benedict; and it is interesting that he continued the Romanesque design, even though by this time Canterbury, from where he came, was using French Gothic in its arcading. The splendid painted ceiling is unique in England and dates from about 1220. The western transepts, west front, and north-west tower were the last parts of the main cathedral structure to be completed, around 1230.

The Galilee porch on the west front was built in 1380 to halt the forward leaning of the central arcade. The so-called 'new building', at the far east end of the cathedral, is of the richest Perpendicular construction and is by John Wastell, who was responsible for the noble Bell Harry Tower at Canterbury. Some of the monastic buildings survive, including the Almoners' and Infirmarers' Halls, the shell of the infirmary itself, and hints of both the cloister and refectory. Among those who were buried in Peterborough Cathedral were Catherine of Aragon (1536) and Mary Queen of Scots (1587), who was later reburied in Westminster Abbey.

The Gothic west front.

ELY CATHEDRAL

The 'Ship of the Fens' rising from the mist is a name and an image often used to describe Ely's majestic cathedral. In earlier times it was not quite a ship, but certainly it crowned an island in the fens, an island famous for its trade in eels. To this island in 673 came Etheldreda to set up her double monastery for men and women. Her shrine was at the centre of the earliest monastic church, which was later destroyed by the Danes in 869. In 970 Benedictine monks re-established an abbey and, in 1083, the octogenarian Abbot Simeon began building the Romanesque church.

Construction of the present church took more than 100 years to complete. The nave foundations were laid in the year 1100, and nine years later the abbey also became a cathedral. By the year 1106, the eastern end was complete and the north and south transepts followed. In the thirteenth century Bishop Northwold rebuilt the east end, adding six bays in the Early English style. The nave remains a good example of Romanesque work with a large triforium and rather simple clerestory.

Two of the remarkable features of Ely Cathedral date from the fourteenth century. The splendid Lady Chapel was completed in 1348 in Decorated style. It is the largest chapel of its kind attached to any British cathedral. In 1322 the central tower collapsed and the unique octagon was conceived by William Hurley, Edward III's master carpenter. The vast space crowned by the octagon was created by taking a bay from each of the four sides.

Sir Gilbert Scott's board ceiling in the nave was built between 1855 and 1858. Few of the domestic monastic buildings have survived – the chapter house and the cloister were destroyed at the time of the Dissolution, though, fortunately, the magnificent twelfth-century Prior's Door into the cloister has survived. Some of the monastic buildings, including the former infirmary, have been converted into domestic dwellings. The north-west transept, flanking the western tower, disappeared during the fifteenth century, but the tower itself and the south-western transept remain as a noble west front, welcoming the pilgrim and visitor. In 2000 a new processional way was completed linking the Lady Chapel with the cathedral crossing. In 2018 new furnishings were completed for the octagon space.

Above: The fourteenth-century octagon.

Ely's west front.

ST EDMUNDSBURY CATHEDRAL

The death of St Edmund, King of the East Angles, in the year 869 was clearly both a traumatic and formative event for this part of England. It is likely that he died close by to the present-day town of Bury St Edmunds. In 1032 a round church was built as a shrine to house St Edmund's remains, which had been kept safely for over 160 years. The abbey was begun during the abbacy of Baldwin, 1065–97; he also built the nearby church of St Denis. Anselm, the abbot from 1121–48, continued the building, making the abbey church the greatest Benedictine foundation in East Anglia, larger even than the cathedral at Norwich. St Denis' Church was demolished to make space for the western transept of the new abbey church.

Anselm, however, also built a new church dedicated to St James, the nave of which was the antecedent of the nave of the present cathedral. In 1503 a new nave was built; its designer was the remarkable John Wastell who lived in Bury. Wastell was the builder of the Bell Harry Tower at Canterbury, and the vaulting and ante-chapel of King's College Chapel in Cambridge. His nave here at Bury has a similar sense of height and nobility. The present nave roof is by Sir George Gilbert Scott (built 1862–64) and the attractive colouring, designed by Stephen Dykes Bower, was added from 1948 to 1982.

Dykes Bower's magnificent additions were made necessary when the church became a cathedral with the creation of the new diocese in 1914. His first new work was the north-west porch and the beginnings of the south walk of the cloister. In 1970 the crossing with its modest transepts and the fine aisled choir were begun. The style, which is twentieth-century Perpendicular, matches the nobility of Wastell's nave. Throughout, the ceilings are splendid in their colouring and there is a magnificent wrought iron screen at the entrance to the Lady Chapel. In 2005, the majestic tower by Hugh Mathew (Dykes Bower's former assistant), was completed. Alongside this was included a north transept, a crypt with a chapel above and the east walk of the cloister. The painted vaulting of the tower was completed in 2010.

The new tower was completed in 2005.

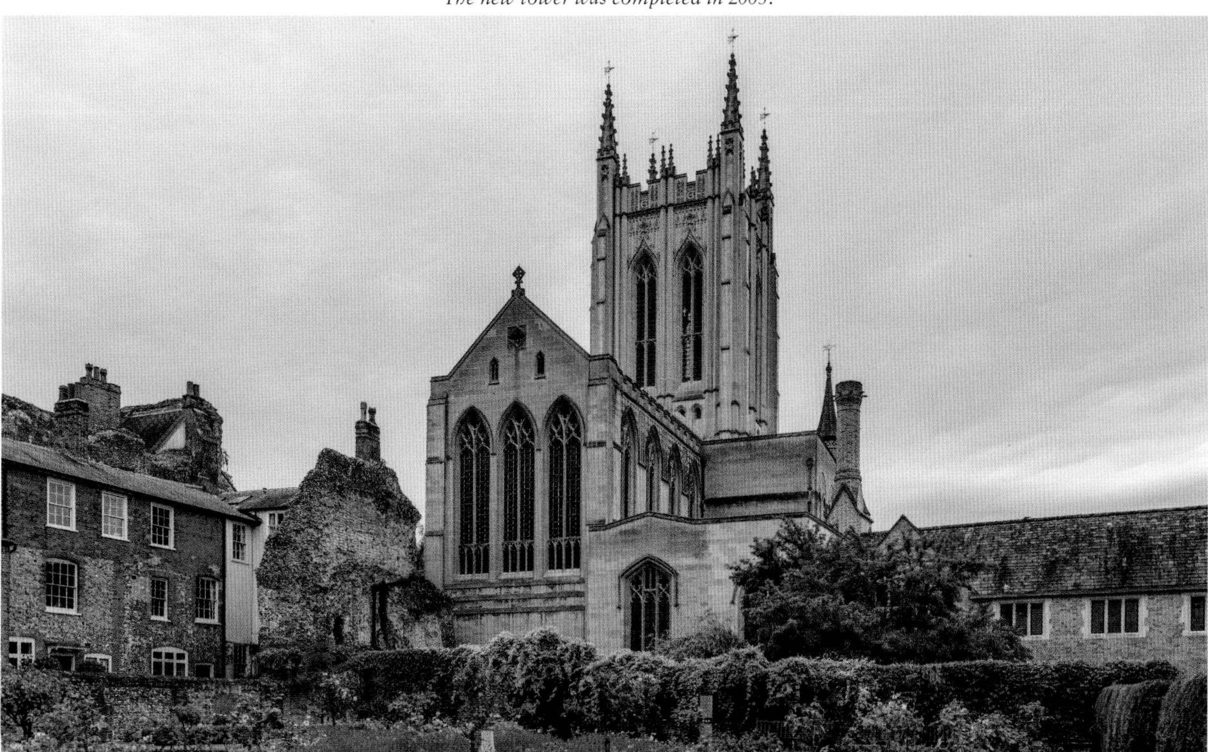

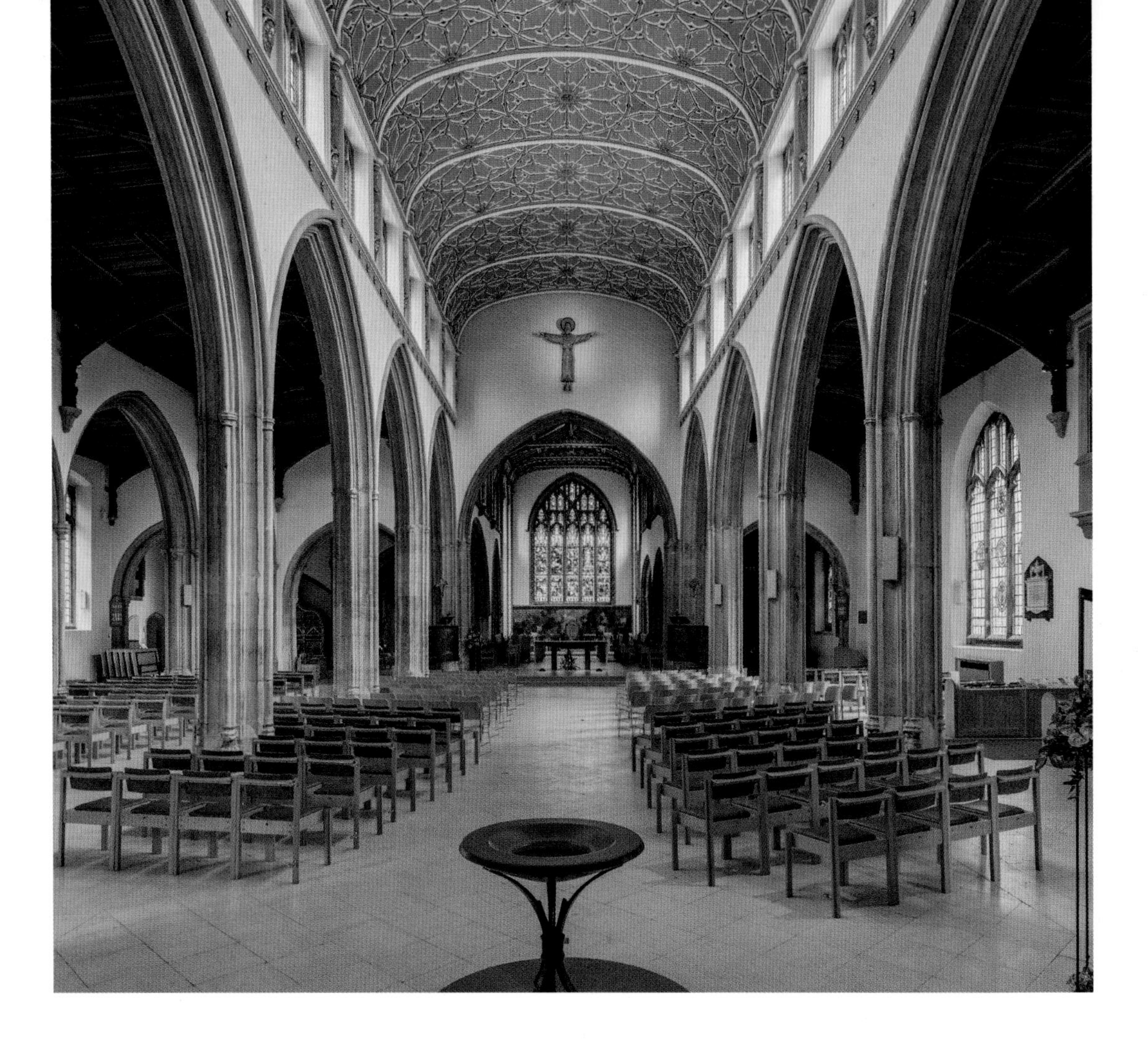

CHELMSFORD CATHEDRAL

In the east of the diocese of Chelmsford, at Bradwell, stands the tiny church of St Peter. Built by St Cedd in the seventh century, it is the oldest stone church in England. This sets the context for the Cathedral Church of St Mary with St Peter and St Cedd in Chelmsford. Chelmsford gained its charter for a market in 1199, but the church of St Mary (as it was then known) came later; the first named incumbent is Richard de Gorges, who was appointed in 1242. The western tower is fifteenth century, the lantern and needle spire being added in 1749. The two-storeyed south porch is also fifteenth century, but the medieval nave collapsed in 1800, after which it was rebuilt, still in Gothic style, and with galleries that were later removed.

The whole cathedral was extensively reordered and refurbished in 1983 when it gained its present feel of grace and space. A new limestone floor was laid and a Westmorland slate altar (by Robert Potter) and bishop's chair (by John Skelton) were placed in the fifteenth-century chancel with its slender arches looking north and south into the aisles. St Cedd's chapel is set aside for private prayer; outside the screen on the north wall is a relief of *Christ the Healer* by Georg Ehrlich. Another Ehrlich relief, *The Bombed Child*, can be seen in the Chapel of St Peter. It reflects the dedication of the chapel to those who suffer 'in this world'. The chapter house was built in 1990. The *Christ in Glory*, by Peter Ball, the *Tree of Life* painting by Mark Cazalet and the Bradwell Chapel tapestry by Philip Sanderson are the most recent additions to this modest, but most elegant, of cathedrals. The St Cedd window in the chapel of that name, designed again by Mark Cazalet, marked the centenary of the diocese in 2014.

Above: The Gothic-style nave.
Opposite: Hereford Cathedral.

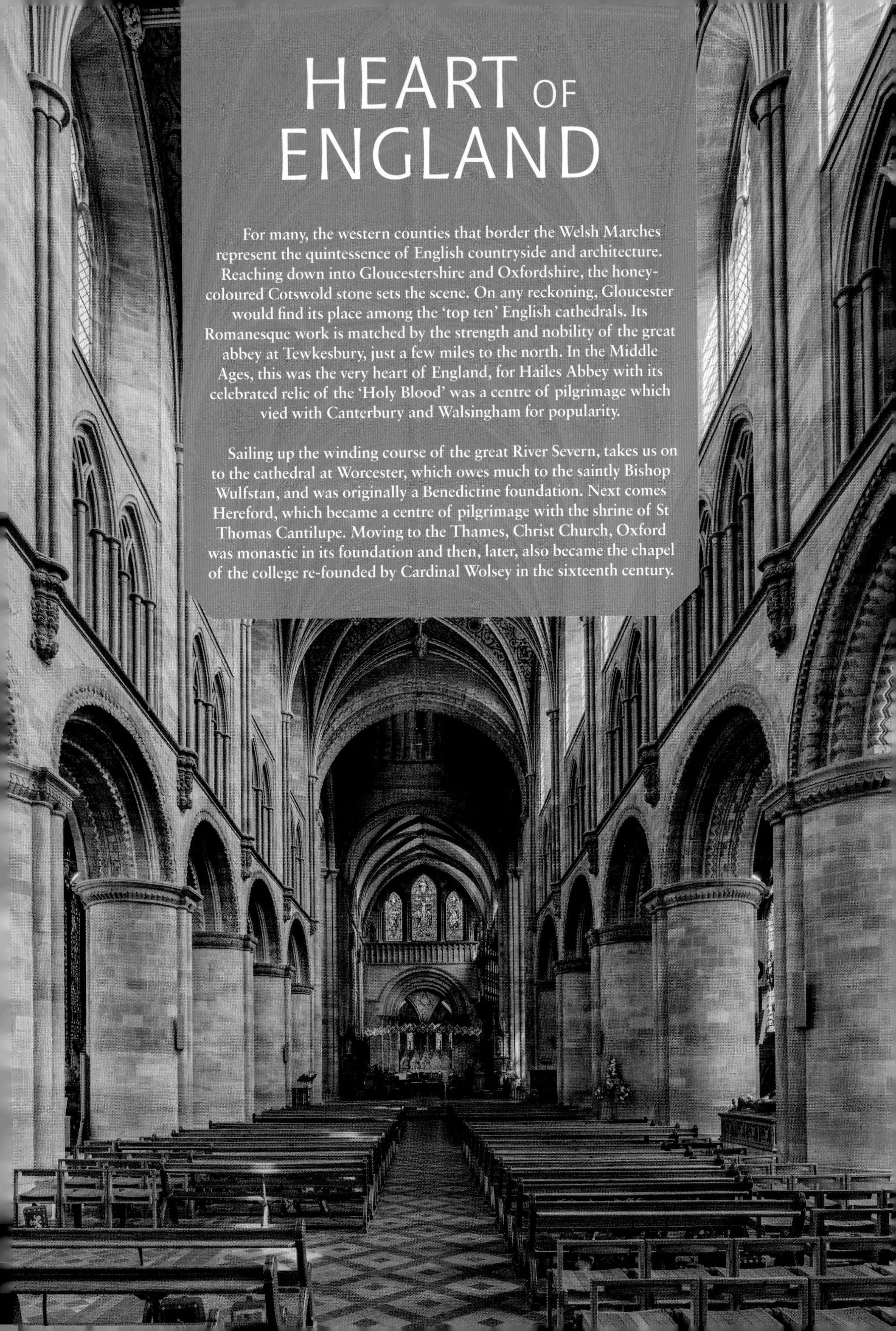

HEART OF ENGLAND

For many, the western counties that border the Welsh Marches represent the quintessence of English countryside and architecture. Reaching down into Gloucestershire and Oxfordshire, the honey-coloured Cotswold stone sets the scene. On any reckoning, Gloucester would find its place among the 'top ten' English cathedrals. Its Romanesque work is matched by the strength and nobility of the great abbey at Tewkesbury, just a few miles to the north. In the Middle Ages, this was the very heart of England, for Hailes Abbey with its celebrated relic of the 'Holy Blood' was a centre of pilgrimage which vied with Canterbury and Walsingham for popularity.

Sailing up the winding course of the great River Severn, takes us on to the cathedral at Worcester, which owes much to the saintly Bishop Wulfstan, and was originally a Benedictine foundation. Next comes Hereford, which became a centre of pilgrimage with the shrine of St Thomas Cantilupe. Moving to the Thames, Christ Church, Oxford was monastic in its foundation and then, later, also became the chapel of the college re-founded by Cardinal Wolsey in the sixteenth century.

WORCESTER CATHEDRAL

Standing proudly above the River Severn, Worcester Cathedral is a symbol of this part of England. The diocese has a long history; the first bishop was Bosel, in 680. In the year 983, the cathedral was established by Bishop Oswald. In 1041 the cathedral was seriously damaged in a Danish raid, but it was not until 1084, with the general initiative of William the Conqueror, that Bishop Wulfstan began the rebuilding. This was started from the east end, and by 1089, the crypt and the area above it was complete; this crypt has survived and it remains the largest Norman crypt in England. Building continued until the Romanesque cathedral was complete. The final two western bays, finished around 1170, are late enough to be in the Transitional style.

Wulfstan's achievement was considerable and he was canonised in 1203. During the thirteenth century, King John was buried in the cathedral (1216) and his noble tomb remains at the centre of the quire. In 1224, Bishop William de Blois began rebuilding in Early English style, beginning with the new Lady Chapel at the east end. He continued to rebuild, moving west through the quire and demolishing Wulfstan's Romanesque cathedral. This work continued throughout the fourteenth century, with a break almost certainly caused by the Black Death. This break is detectable since the earlier work is Decorated, while the later southern arcades of the nave are Perpendicular in style. The splendid crossing, tower and great transept were completed, also in the Perpendicular style, by 1374.

The north porch was completed in 1386, and the remarkable and elaborate chantry to Prince Arthur, the older brother of King Henry VIII, was completed in the period after his death in 1502. Amongst the monastic buildings to survive is the chapter house with its banded green and white stone and one central supporting column, and also a fine cloister rebuilt at the end of the fourteenth and the beginning of the fifteenth century. Recent excavation has shown that the chapter house was built over the cemetery of the Anglo-Saxon cathedral. The monks' refectory also survived and became College Hall, which is now used by the King's School.

The cloister.

HEREFORD CATHEDRAL

The beginnings of the diocese and cathedral at Hereford take us back to the year 676 when Putta was made the first bishop. There has possibly been a cathedral on the present site since the late seventh century. The Normans rebuilt the cathedral, and substantial elements of this Romanesque building have survived, including the south transept, much of the crossing and choir, and the main aisle of the nave.

In the thirteenth century the cathedral was transformed by the introduction of the Early English style. An ambulatory was built at the eastern end, together with a Lady Chapel constructed over a crypt, an arrangement unique at this time in England. The north transept was built around 1250, using Purbeck marble and acute Gothic arches, mirroring those in Westminster Abbey, which date from the same period. A ten-sided chapter house was also built during this time, the ruins of which can still be seen.

Above: Viewed from the north west.

The splendid dignity of the central tower owes its origins to the fourteenth century, and notably to the gifts received from pilgrims following the death of St Thomas Cantilupe in 1282. Cantilupe was a pious, learned and courageous bishop. He defended his own diocesan jurisdiction in the face of John Peckham, Archbishop of Canterbury, and indeed died while pursuing his cause at the Papal Court. The shrine of St Thomas Cantilupe has recently been restored with great flourish and colour.

The fifteenth century saw the construction of the delightful college of the Vicars Choral in 1475. The only surviving parallels to this beautiful collection of buildings overlooking the River Wye are at St George's Chapel, Windsor and at Wells Cathedral. In 1480, the splendid fan-vaulted Stanbury Chantry was completed. The eighteenth and nineteenth centuries saw substantial restorations. James Wyatt rebuilt the west end of the nave, following a collapse in 1786, and the Victorian restoration dates from 1840–63.

Hereford has some remarkable treasures, including the Mappa Mundi (*c*. 1300), a Limoges reliquary of Thomas Becket, the eighth-century Hereford Gospels and the Chained Library, the furnishing of which dates from 1611. The Mappa Mundi and the Chained Library are housed in the refurbished cloister and in a fine library building designed by Sir William Whitfield and completed in 1996. Most recently John Maine has designed the new Special Air Service window and sculpture which he has called *Ascension*.

The choir and the corona.

GLOUCESTER CATHEDRAL

Gloucester Cathedral is a building of dazzling beauty. The contrast between the clear robust splendour of the Romanesque nave and the intricacy of the Perpendicular choir, presbytery, tower and Lady Chapel is unforgettable. The origins of the cathedral reach back into the seventh century when King Osric of Mercia established a monastery here in 679. During the reign of Cnut, the monastery was taken from the secular priests and handed over to Benedictine monks. It was the arrival of the Normans, however, that presaged the building of the earliest parts of the cathedral which are still visible today. The foundation stone of the new abbey church was laid in 1089. In 1541 King Henry VIII founded a new diocese and the abbey became a cathedral.

The fine Romanesque nave was not completed until *c.* 1126. The architecture is simple without being severe, robust and yet still graceful. The strong and plain circular columns reflect a pattern resonant with other churches in the Severn Valley. The decoration of the arches uses the restrained dog-tooth patterns characteristic of Norman work; the triforium above is low, owing to the scale of the main arcades. During this period there was internecine strife between the sons of William the Conqueror. Robert Curthose, the eldest son, who had hoped to succeed to the throne, was held captive in Cardiff Castle for many years and eventually buried in the chapter house of the Abbey of St Peter, Gloucester. His wooden effigy is now in the south ambulatory of the choir. The Romanesque nave is crowned with a beautiful plain Early English vault of 1242.

Gloucester preserves the clear patterns of the former Benedictine monastery perhaps better than any other English cathedral, since many of the pre-Reformation monastic buildings survive. This is also true of the church itself. The clear division between the nave, or people's church, and the choir, or monks' church, is still there – now delineated by an early nineteenth-century choir screen. To move into the choir and presbytery is to move into a different world, not only because of its monastic origins but because the architecture, for the choir,

Tower from the cloisters.

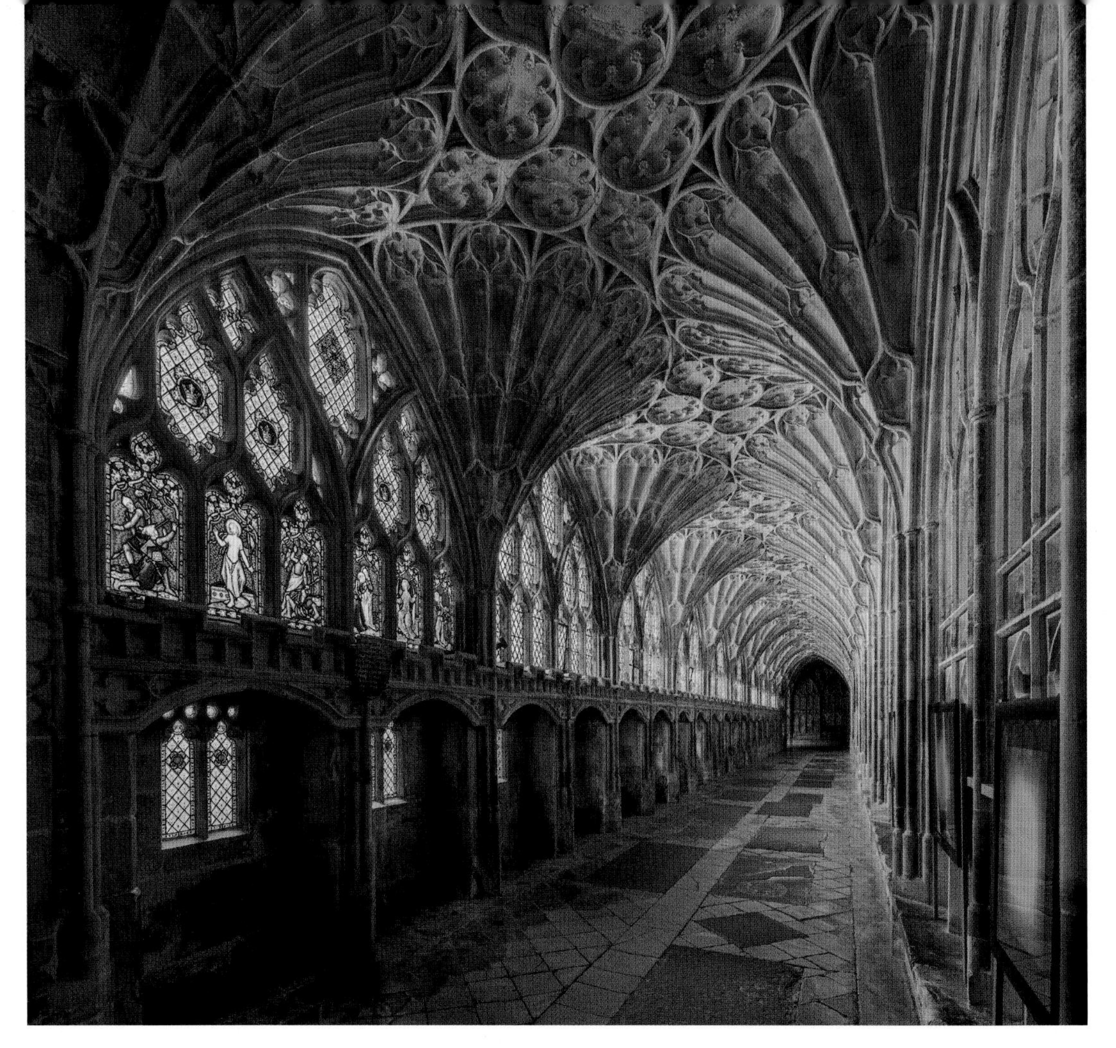

The cloister's glorious fan vaulting.

transepts and presbytery are examples of the earliest and most beautiful Perpendicular work in England.

The original Norman east end would have been fairly dark, but the vaulting, windows, and tracery – all built after the murder of Edward II, whose majestic tomb is in the north ambulatory – give a feeling of light, space and height. The great east window is one of the wonders of Gloucester. It is effectively a great glass reredos depicting the medieval hierarchy with angels in the top panels, Christ, Mary and the saints in the upper ones, and knights and bishops at the bottom. Many of the knights commemorated fought at the Battle of Crécy of 1346. In contrast to this medieval glass, nearby in the south ambulatory is the fine Thomas Denny window of 1993, *The Risen Christ*. There is also some good nineteenth-century glass by C.E. Kempe on the north and south sides of the ambulatory. The lierne vaulting of the presbytery is covered with bosses and this part of the cathedral reaches remarkable conclusions in both the east and the west. In the west, flying spans carry the springing for the last bay of the vault. In the east there is a passage linking both the north and south sides, known as the Whispering Gallery.

The Lady Chapel, begun in 1470, is a stunning conclusion to the building. It is unusual in having chantry chapels to both south and north with singing galleries above them. The chantries have fan-vaulting, but the Lady Chapel itself has a lierne vault, similar to that in the choir, with parallel ridge-ribs. The chapel, which was badly damaged after the Reformation, contains magnificent glass by the Arts and Crafts artist Christopher Whall, completed in 1905 and three paintings by Iain McKillop, depicting the crucifixion, deposition and resurrection of Jesus Christ, painted in 2003 and sensitively placed on the damaged medieval reredos.

The great cloister is arguably the most beautiful cloister in England. It was begun in the 1360s and completed very early in the fifteenth century, and the fan-vaulting is one of the glories of this period. The tower, also Perpendicular, is from the mid-fifteenth century. The first stage of Gloucester's Pilgrim Project has been completed with the landscaping of the new cathedral green.

CHRIST CHURCH CATHEDRAL, OXFORD

Christ Church, Oxford is unique among English cathedrals, being both a cathedral and a college chapel. Approached from St Aldates through the magnificent Tom Quad, begun by Cardinal Wolsey in 1524, the noble Tom Tower was added by Sir Christopher Wren in 1682. To make room for the quad buildings, the priory church (now the cathedral) was substantially foreshortened. Although comparatively small, it is nevertheless a treasure house historically and architecturally.

The early history is dominated by the legend of St Frideswide. Whether she founded the monastery that preceded the later Augustinian foundation is uncertain; her death in October 727, however, is attested from the twelfth century, and her burial place was probably in or near the north-eastern side of the present cathedral. Her shrine base was returned here and beautifully restored in 2002. Oxford's origins may be traced to this early Saxon nunnery, which was burned to the ground in 1002 with some 600 local Danes inside, an early act of ethnic cleansing instigated by King Aethelred who penitently rebuilt the church in 1004.

At the beginning of the twelfth century the monastery was re-founded for Augustinian canons. Prior Robert of Cricklade established the plan of the present church, chapter house and cloister, finishing his chancel in 1170, and the crossing tower with its aisled transepts some 15 years later. The cathedral spire (one of England's earliest) dates from *c.* 1230, as does the Lady Chapel. The Latin Chapel was completed in 1338. Near these now stands a Peace and Reconciliation chapel in memory of Bishop George Bell: the cruciform altar by Jim Partridge is made of Windsor oak given by Her Majesty The Queen.

William Orchard's superb lierne quire vaulting

Above: Sanctuary and pendant vaulting.

Above: Viewed from Christ Church meadow.
Opposite: St Paul's Cathedral, London.

with its elegant pendants dates from *c.* 1500. The only other monastic buildings surviving are the Prior's Lodging and parts of the old dormitory and refectory (now Priory House). The fine Early English chapter house (1220–40) has some splendid interior carving.

Much of the stained glass is of exceptional quality and variety. The Becket window was made in 1320. Two windows and parts of others are by the seventeenth-century Flemish glazier brothers, Van Linge. Four windows by Sir Edward Burne-Jones and made by William Morris are from the 1870s, but Burne-Jones' Frideswide window (1859) in the Latin Chapel is in his quite different early style.

LONDON AND THE SOUTH-EAST

Augustine's arrival in Kent in 597 marked the beginnings of the English Church as it exists today. Not only did Augustine build a cathedral, he also established the abbey nearby, which bears his name. The advance of his mission to Rochester and then to London led to the beginnings of Rochester Cathedral, and St Paul's Cathedral in London around 604. This part of England, however, bears the marks of an even earlier Christian mission with the martyrdom of St Alban in the third century.

Battle Abbey in Sussex reminds us of the Norman invasion of Britain, which left its mark upon a number of English cathedrals and abbeys, not least in the South-East. Some of the earliest Norman or Romanesque work in England is seen in the transepts and nave of St Albans Cathedral. The transepts in Winchester, the east end of Canterbury, and parts of Rochester are other examples. There is also the splendid neo-Byzantine Westminster Cathedral and the modern Gothic of Guildford Cathedral.

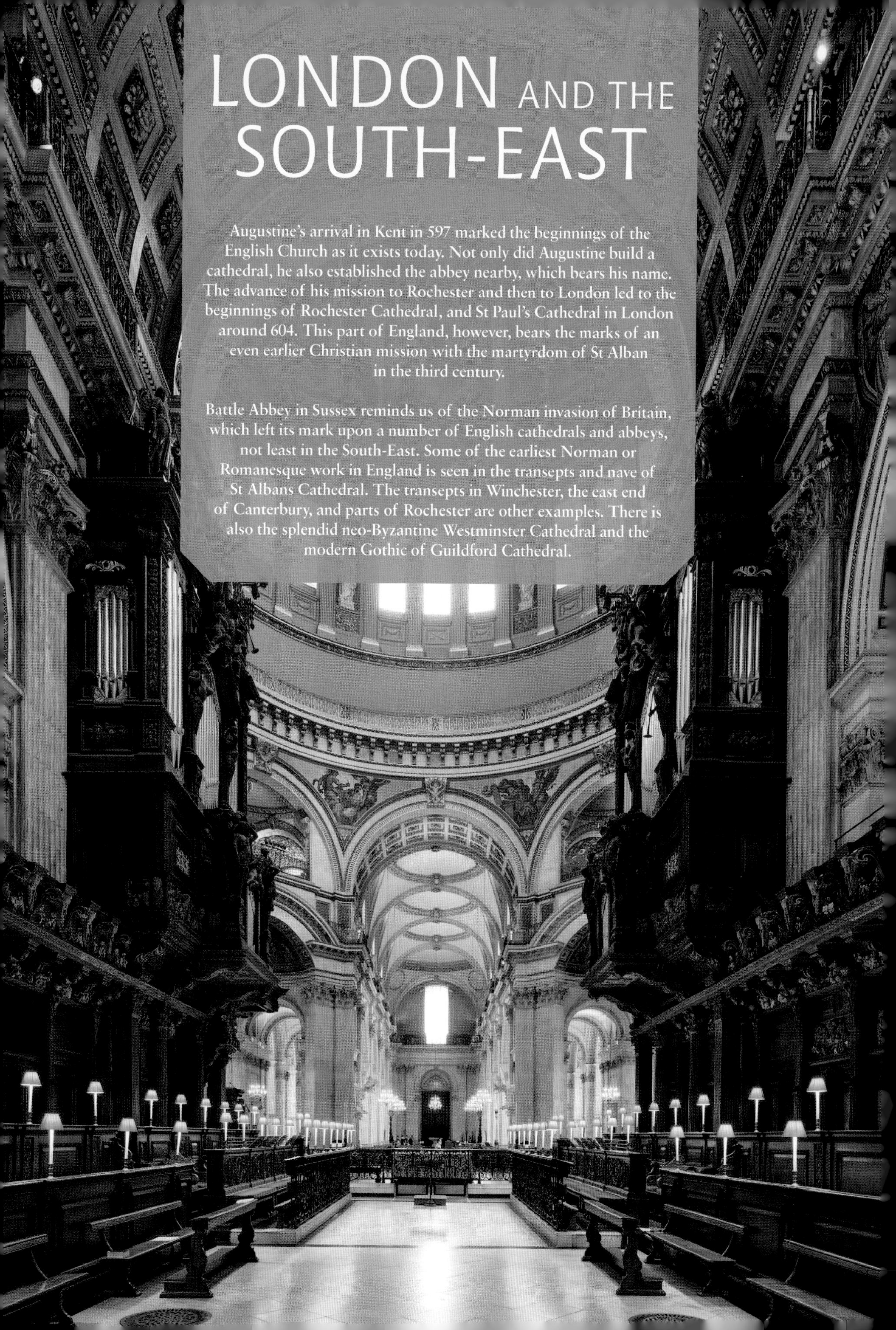

ST ALBANS CATHEDRAL

The strong and austere tower of the Cathedral and Abbey Church of St Alban, boasting Roman brick in its construction, focuses the unique interest of this historic place. Here, outside the ancient Roman city of Verulamium, in the mid-third century, Alban became the first Christian martyr of this land. There was a shrine here as early as 429, and in the eighth century Bede wrote that here 'a beautiful church worthy of [Alban's] martyrdom was built'. In 793 King Offa of Mercia established a Benedictine double monastery for men and women, and in 960 it was re-founded with a stricter Benedictine discipline.

The present church was begun in 1077; from the beginning the monastery was conceived on a grand scale. All that now remains, following the Dissolution of the Monasteries, is the gatehouse and the abbey church. Approaching from the gatehouse it is easy to appreciate both the scale and significance of Lord Grimthorpe's nineteenth-century restoration, when the west front was completely rebuilt. The nave, at 84 metres (275 feet), is the longest in England. The four western bays were extended in 1190 in Early English style, while the easternmost arcades are Romanesque, with plaster covering Roman brick. After their collapse in 1323, the four bays of the south nave aisle arcade were reconstructed in the Decorated style.

The nave is separated from the choir and presbytery by a stone screen, beyond which was the monks' church. The choir and transepts include much Romanesque work, but the end wall of the south transept was rebuilt in the 1880s. Beyond the fine high altar screen of 1484, restored by Lord Aldenham in the 1890s, is the shrine of St Alban. The pedestal of the shrine, dated 1308, was magnificently restored in 1991. Still further east is the Lady Chapel, completed in 1320. For 300 years it was walled off from the rest of the cathedral and used by St Albans School.

The chapter house, designed by Sir William Whitfield and using modernised Romanesque forms, opened in 1982. Including a library, song school and refectory, the choir now process into the cathedral from the chapter house using the Michael Stair, a dramatic gallery and staircase modelled on a medieval night stair. The newest additions are the sculptures now placed in the nave sanctuary.

Above: St Albans' long nave from the west.
Opposite: The choir showing painted ceiling and Romanesque arcades.

ARUNDEL CATHEDRAL

As with the Roman Catholic cathedral in Norwich, so in Arundel the building was made possible through the generosity of the 15th Duke of Norfolk. It is a magnificent example of nineteenth-century Gothic Revival in the French style of around 1400. The architect was Joseph Hansom, who designed Birmingham Town Hall and the Hansom Cab.

Arundel Cathedral exudes a sense of height, both inside and out. It has an aisled nave of six bays and is cruciform in plan with an apsidal sanctuary, again following the style of French Gothic. In the nave the arcades with their slender columns and pointed arches add to the sense of height. In the north transept are the remains of St Philip Howard, Earl of Arundel, who was martyred in 1595 during the reign of Queen Elizabeth I. There is a noble western gallery, housing the organ, and beyond that a fine rose window.

Right: Arundel's aisled nave.

ST PAUL'S CATHEDRAL

Augustine's mission to Kent in 597 meant that in England, following the Roman pattern, dioceses began to be set up in established cities. Only seven years after Augustine's arrival, Mellitus adopted this pattern and established the first church of St Paul in London in 604; it was wooden and was destroyed and rebuilt several times before a Norman church was constructed on the same site nearly 500 years later, in 1087. This church eventually evolved into the great Gothic building that preceded Wren's masterpiece. Old St Paul's was the largest church in the British Isles and the third largest in medieval Europe, with the tallest spire ever built in England; even the tower pillars, which Wren had to demolish, were more than 61 metres (200 feet) high. The Great Fire of London in 1666 finally put paid to this ancient building.

Christopher Wren's sublime new cathedral reflected the contemporary interest in Classical architecture and was built in English Baroque. Constructed between 1675 and 1710, it is dominated by the magnificent dome, which is 111 metres (365 feet) high to the top of the cross which surmounts it. The dome has become a symbol of the City of London. The cathedral was built using stone from the royal quarries at Portland in Dorset. The west front has a pediment which includes a bas-relief of the conversion of St Paul, and this is crowned with a statue of the saint flanked by figures of St Peter and St James. The twin towers of the west front house the bells and the clock, including the largest bell, Great Paul, which weighs 17 tonnes.

The cathedral is entered through the west front. At the bottom of the famous steps is a statue of Queen Anne (the reigning monarch when the cathedral was completed). The building is broad and cruciform in plan. The view down the wide

From the southeast with the tower of the ruined St Augustine's church.

The choir and baldachino.

nave and beyond the crossing is rich and splendid, with the fine mosaics on the ceiling of the quire, and the great baldachino fixing one's gaze at the far end. The Classical arcading of the nave breathes an atmosphere of splendour and strength. In the western bay of the nave is the Italian marble font, which dates from 1727. The nave is flanked by north and south aisles. In the north aisle is Alfred Stevens' towering monument to the Duke of Wellington; at the far west end is the chapel of St Dunstan, decorated after the manner of Raphael. At the west end of the south aisle is the chapel of the Order of St Michael and St George, an order with strong links with the diplomatic service.

Moving further east, the transepts are again broad. Also here is one of the three versions of William Holman-Hunt's famous painting *The Light of the World*. In the south transept is John Flaxman's monument to Admiral Horatio Nelson, whose tomb is in the centre of the crypt. The dome encloses a vast space at the crossing which is paved in black and white marble, and at the centre is the Latin epitaph to Wren which includes the famous phrase: '... if you seek his monument, look around you.' The dome is among the largest in the world and contains the famous Whispering Gallery. The dome's frescoes, depicting the life of St Paul, were painted by Sir James Thornhill between 1716 and 1719.

The magnificent baldachino in the quire is modern (1958) and surmounts an altar of Italian marble; this replaces earlier work lost through bomb damage. The very fine choir stalls are, like much of the other carving, by the seventeenth-century Dutch master, Grinling Gibbons. In the ambulatory is Henry Moore's fine modern sculpture, *Mother and Child*. The Lady Chapel, in the south-eastern corner of the cathedral, was dedicated, in 1959, to the Blessed Virgin Mary. The Chapel of Modern Martyrs commemorates all known Anglican martyrs who have died for their faith since 1850.

Finally, descending to the crypt, we enter another remarkable world. Although it is the largest crypt in Europe, it is graceful in its architectural style. The Winston Churchill Gates across the crypt, by James Horrobin, were completed in 2004. Wellington is buried here alongside Nelson, and there are memorials to a number of distinguished contributors to the arts, including Henry Moore, Sir Edwin Lutyens, Sir Arthur Sullivan and William Blake. The Chapel of the Order of the British Empire is also here, as is the cathedral's Treasury. Recent years have seen a remarkable stone cleaning project and both the cathedral's interior and exterior now reflect Wren's original vision. Bill Viola's two video installations *Mary* and *Martyrs* are St Paul's most recent art commissions.

WESTMINSTER CATHEDRAL

For the average explorer of English cathedrals and churches, to enter John Francis Bentley's basilican Westminster Cathedral is to enter a new world. The sense of 'mystical space' together with the lofty dark domes, marble and mosaics is more familiar to the traveller in Ravenna or Istanbul. Cardinal Vaughan (1832–1903), whose energy made possible the construction of this remarkable building, was clear that he did not want Gothic; his intention had been that the cathedral should be a Roman-style basilica, and so Bentley's Byzantine solution was a surprise even to him.

The nave is both the highest and broadest in the country, giving an unimpeded view of the high altar, which stands beneath a majestic baldachino of Verona marble. There are transepts, but these are cleverly caught up architecturally into the basilical space. Building began in 1895 and the cathedral was consecrated in 1910. The nave consists of three square bays crowned with domes; this structure is supported by a series of subsidiary side arches. The nave piers are covered in dark green marble from Thessaly in northern Greece; the same marble was used centuries ago for the decoration of Hagia Sophia in Constantinople (Istanbul).

The sanctuary is marked off from the nave space by a 9-metre (30-foot) high hanging rood crucifix by Christian Symons. Mounted on the nave piers are the magnificent Stations of the Cross by Eric Gill. The sense of journey often experienced when moving from nave to sanctuary in a Gothic church is not lost, but is replaced by a similar progression via the side chapels; it is a journey from birth to death, beginning at the baptistry in the south-west corner, as one enters, and ending with the Chapel of the Holy Souls in the cathedral's north-west corner. There is a shrine to St John Southworth, a Reformation martyr, in the chapel of St George and the English Martyrs. Cardinal Basil Hume was interred in the Chapel of St Gregory in 1999.

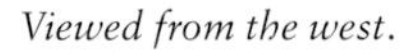

Viewed from the west.

SOUTHWARK CATHEDRAL

At the heart of London's regenerated Bankside, Southwark Cathedral is an architectural gem. There has been a church here for over 1,000 years, the original having been built over a Roman villa (Southwark was a suburb of Londinium). In the mid-ninth century St Swithun, Bishop of Winchester, within whose diocese it lay, set up a college of priests, and there are still some ruins of a palace of the bishops of Winchester nearby. In Edward the Confessor's time a monastery was established here.

The origins of the present church lie in the foundation of a priory of Augustinian canons set up to serve the new church of St Mary Overie (over the river) in the year 1106; the same canons set up St Thomas' Hospital. Very few traces of this original Norman work survive, due to a serious fire in 1212. The church was rebuilt between 1220 and 1273; the fine Early English work in the quire, retro-quire and quire aisles dates from this period. Also completed then were the lower parts of the tower and the western bays of the nave. In 1283 construction resumed and the main structure, including the nave and transepts, was finished by the mid-fourteenth century. Disaster struck again in the 1390s with another fire, but by 1420 the rebuilding was complete; this included the remainder of the tower and the rebuilding of the south transept.

In 1469 the nave roof collapsed, leading to further rebuilding. The magnificent Perpendicular screen between the high altar and the retro-quire was given by Richard Fox, the then Bishop of Winchester, in 1520. After the Reformation, the priory having been dissolved, the church became the parish church of St Saviour. John Harvard was baptised here in 1607 and is commemorated in the Harvard Chapel, and Lancelot Andrewes, the saintly bishop of Winchester, is buried in the cathedral. In 1890 the foundation stone was laid of the present Victorian Gothic nave. The diocese of Southwark was carved out of the diocese of Winchester in 1905 and the church became a cathedral. In 2001, Dr Nelson Mandela opened the cathedral's Millennium Buildings, the work of the architectural practice of Richard Griffiths, and comprising shop, refectory, library and conference rooms.

Above: The choir vault.

ROCHESTER CATHEDRAL

After Canterbury, Rochester is the oldest diocese in England, Augustine having sent one of his fellow monks there to be the first bishop in 604. The mortal remains of Paulinus, the great missionary to Northumbria, are still in this cathedral. Nothing is visible of the Saxon cathedral, and it is the church begun by the Norman bishop, Gundulf, in 1077 of which the earliest remains are visible. Gundulf founded a Benedictine community and set to work on a new Romanesque church. Parts of his cathedral are still visible in the nave arcading, the western part of the crypt and in his tower on the north side of the cathedral. The magnificent Romanesque western facade was completed around 1160. The remains of the monastic cloister and chapter house are from the period 1115–37.

The earliest Gothic work, begun around 1180, can be traced in the enlarged choir, completed with its perfect Early English vault in 1227. During this period a square-ended presbytery was added, without aisles or ambulatory. The broad quire transepts were also built at this time and work continued westwards into the nave, with the complete rebuilding of the first two bays. The north and south nave transepts (including in the north transept some of the best Gothic work in the cathedral) were constructed in the mid to late thirteenth century.

The central tower and spire, completed in 1345, were the work of Bishop Hamo de Hythe. The fifteenth century saw the addition of the great west window, placed in the centre of the Romanesque facade. At the Reformation, Rochester produced two martyrs: Bishop John Fisher for the Catholic cause was beheaded by King Henry VIII in 1535 and Bishop Nicholas Ridley was burned at the stake as a Protestant martyr during the reign of Mary Tudor. Ridley is commemorated in the quire screen.

The baptistry fresco by Sergei Fyodorov (2004) is the first to be painted in an English cathedral for over 800 years. In 2016 the crypt was transformed into an impressive exhibition area.

Above: The west front.

CANTERBURY CATHEDRAL

Canterbury is incomparable, for it is both the shrine to the birth of English Christianity and also the beating heart of the Anglican Communion. It was Thomas Becket's murder in 1170 within the cathedral by four knights of the court of King Henry II that would make Canterbury, along with Compostela, one of the holiest shrines of medieval Europe. But Canterbury's history goes back well beyond Becket's martyrdom, for it was to the court of King Ethelbert of Kent that Pope Gregory sent Augustine in 597. Augustine came to a city where there were already Christian churches, so the cathedral may have been built on the foundation of an earlier church. Something of this continuity was further pressed home when the nave floor was re-paved in 1993, and the foundations of a Saxon cathedral were discovered.

Canterbury sits regally in low-lying land. Its two western towers and the majestic Bell Harry Tower at its centre lift the heart. The cathedral precincts are entered through the Christ Church Gate beneath the sculpture of Christ by Klaus Ringwald. The Perpendicular south-west tower was built in the 1420s by Thomas Mapilton, but the north-west tower, a copy of Mapilton's work, was built in the 1830s when the original Norman tower at last began to crumble.

The early Gothic choir.

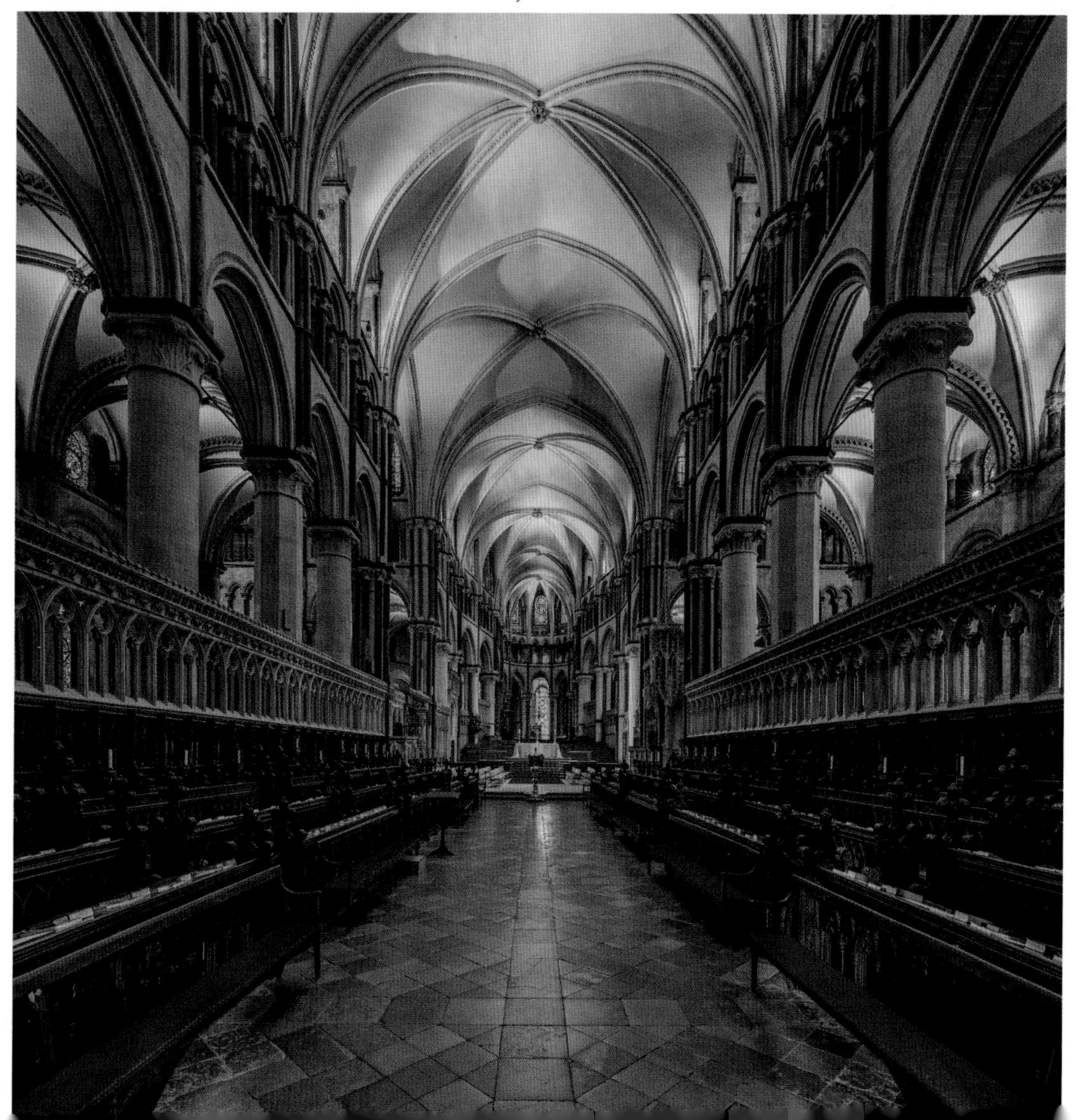

The cloister.

Entering Henry Yevele's breathtaking late fourteenth-century nave is a truly inspiring experience. Its Perpendicular piers are of immense height; the canopied vaulting is spectacular, as, indeed, is the sheer sense of space. To the north of the crossing is the 'Martyrdom', the site of Becket's untimely death. The crossing itself is a place of high architectural drama. Well-worn steps lead up to the pulpitum screen and high above is the dazzling fan-vaulting of the Bell Harry Tower.

The broad quire lies behind the pulpitum, and at the eastern end, behind the high altar, is the thirteenth-century Purbeck 'Chair of St Augustine'. The chair was moved here from the Corona Chapel in July 1977. It reminds pilgrims, and all who come, of the focal role of the Archbishop of Canterbury, not only in the Church of England, but in the worldwide Anglican Communion.

The quire at Canterbury is an unusual piece of very early Gothic; it is almost possible to feel the transition taking place between Romanesque and incipient Gothic. Behind the high altar is the Trinity Chapel, the ultimate destination of medieval pilgrims; it was here that the relics of Becket were translated in the earlier thirteenth century and placed in the heart of a magnificent shrine. The building of the choir began almost immediately after Becket's martyrdom. The builder was William of Sens, who had been brought directly from his work on the new cathedral at Sens in France. In 1538 the agents of Henry VIII dismantled the shrine brutally, beyond any possibility of reconstruction.

At the far east end of the cathedral, beyond the Trinity Chapel, lies the Corona Chapel, now dedicated to the memory of twentieth-century martyrs.

Canterbury may be regarded as a great monastic church. Augustine, like his patron Pope Gregory the Great, was a monk, and Canterbury grew to be a great Benedictine foundation, with over 80 monks.

A walk through the precincts to the north of the cathedral will give a fairly clear picture of the old monastic buildings. The dark entry is surmounted by a canon's house and to the west is the cloister around which the monastic buildings, including the refectory and the dormitories, would have been clustered. The chapter house survives, and immediately beneath the east end of the cathedral is the vast crypt, including the Black Prince's chantry chapel and, at its centre, a Lady Chapel.

From the outside of the cathedral, it is possible to sense the development of the building, with fragments of Romanesque surviving in the east which then grow into early Gothic. The Bell Harry Tower and the nave complete the picture showing later Perpendicular work. Just to the south of the cathedral stands Sir William Whitfield's impressive education centre completed in 2000. The close proximity of St Augustine's Abbey and of the King's School, together with the cathedral's monastic ruins, emphasize the historic and central part that Canterbury has played in the development of Christianity in England.

GUILDFORD CATHEDRAL

The only new cathedral to be built in the province of Canterbury during the twentieth century commands a magnificent site to the north-west of Guildford. The ground crowning Stag Hill was given by the Earl of Onslow as a site for the cathedral of the diocese, which was formed out of part of Winchester diocese in 1927. The building began in 1936, was halted by the outbreak of war three years later, and was resumed in 1952. It was finally consecrated in 1961.

The cathedral, built of modern materials, is clad on the outside mainly with brick with some Clipsham stone from Lincolnshire, and on the inside with plaster and Doulting stone from Somerset. The style is modernised Gothic with soaring pointed arches, giving the fine interior a sense of dignified austerity. Dedicated to the Holy Spirit, the nave arches reach upward, witness to the mystery of God, as intended by Sir Edward Maufe, the architect. The cathedral is of a cruciform plan with narrow transepts and a narthex, the two arms of which extend at the west front.

The nave of seven bays has a floor of Travertine stone with its arches clad in Doulting stone and plaster. The vistas are completely open, with one's eyes being carried directly to the great golden dorsal curtain which is 14 metres (45 feet) high and is surmounted by the rose window by Moira Forsyth. The window depicts the dove descending, and the gifts of the Holy Spirit. At the western end of the south aisle is the baptistry with a font made also of Travertine stone. The organ fills the north transept, and beyond the high altar is the Lady Chapel. There is also a regimental chapel and a modern chapter house.

The exterior mass of the cathedral powerfully dominates Stag Hill, culminating in the strong central tower, which is crowned with a golden angel facing in the direction of the prevailing wind. The cathedral setting within a broad grassland area gives a good, clear sense of space. The building is now flanked by the University of Surrey, creating a link with the city and bringing together the civic, the intellectual and the spiritual life of Guildford. Plans are still to be explored to provide more housing around the cathedral to integrate it more effectively with the rest of the city.

The seven-bayed nave.

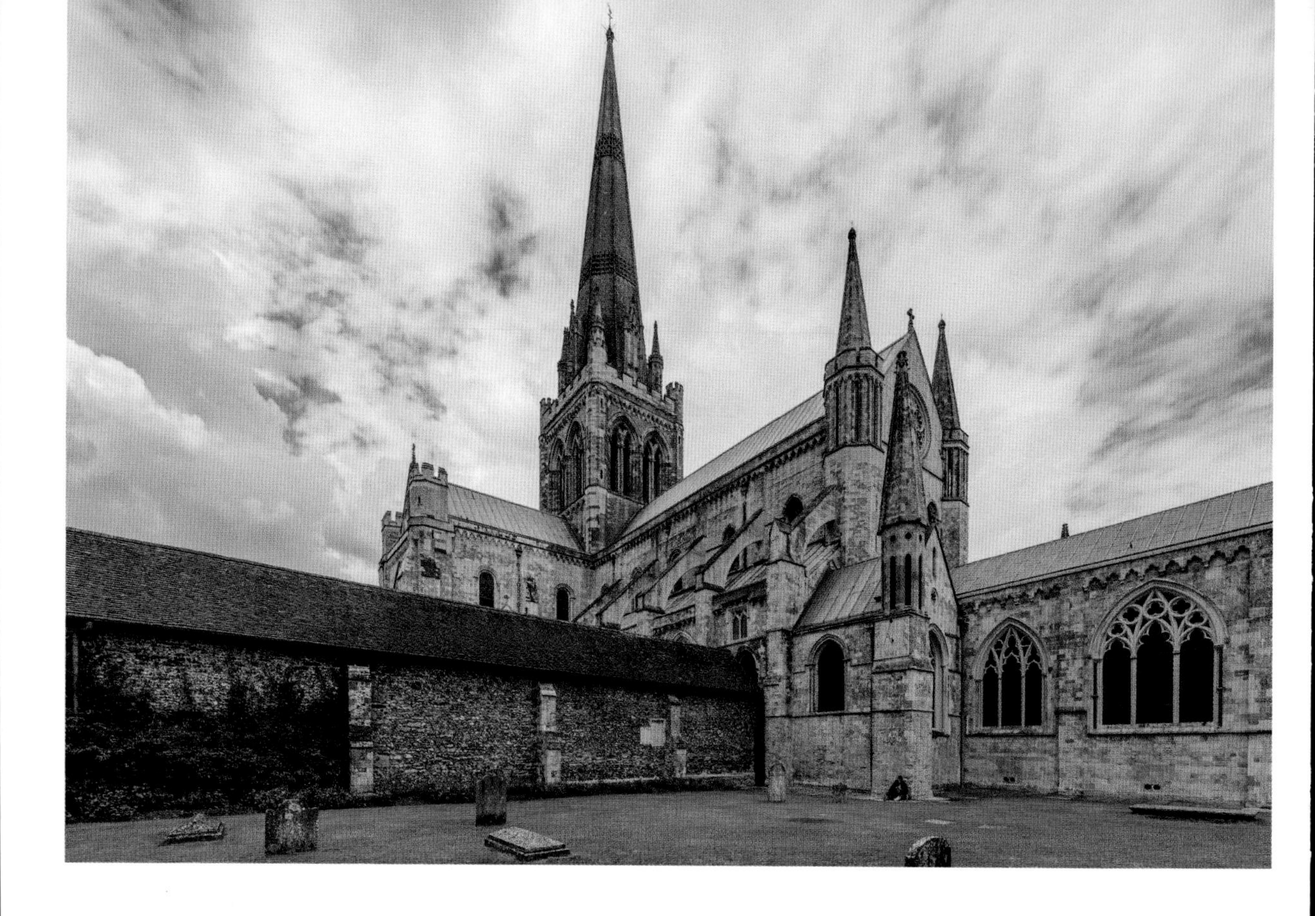

CHICHESTER CATHEDRAL

Wilfrid was one of the most determined of the early missionaries in Anglo-Saxon England. His determination, however, also provoked opposition, and it was exile from Northumbria that brought Wilfrid to the southern Saxons. He set up a cathedral in Selsey in 681, where it remained for 400 years. Following their conquest in 1066, the Normans moved the cathedral to the former Roman town now known as Chichester. This was in 1075, and construction began soon after.

It was Bishops Stigand and Luffa who built the main structure of the cathedral as we see it now. By 1123 the nave, transepts, choir and eastern chapels were largely complete. The Romanesque building was formally dedicated in 1108. In 1187 a fire extensively damaged the east end of the building and the apse was replaced with a two bay retro-choir in the Transitional style. The three eastern bays of the Lady Chapel were added around 1300 in the Decorated style, with vaulting.

The episcopate of Richard of Wych (St Richard of Chichester), 1245–53, was significant because of his pastoral zeal; following his canonisation a shrine was set up in the retro-choir. Destroyed at the Reformation, the site has now regained its significance as a destination for pilgrims.

The beginning of the fifteenth century saw renewed building activity with the addition of the spire, the cloisters in Perpendicular style and the detached bell tower, the survival of which is unique among English cathedrals. At around the same time the interior was enhanced by the construction of a magnificent stone pulpitum; this was removed in the nineteenth century, but happily rebuilt and restored in memory of Bishop George Bell in 1961. This restoration was the initiative of Dean Walter Hussey, who commissioned work by some fine twentieth-century artists. Examples include Graham Sutherland's painting *Noli me tangere* (1961), John Piper's striking tapestry behind the high altar (1966) and stained glass by Marc Chagall (1978). The introduction of contemporary art continues: recent examples are a statue of St Richard by Philip Jackson (2000) and an icon, also of St Richard, by Sergei Fyodorov (2003).

Above: Viewed from the south east.

PORTSMOUTH CATHEDRAL

The naval tradition of the city of Portsmouth has coloured this delightful cathedral. Its tower and lantern have long been signals of homecoming to seamen over the centuries. Since 1984 the grave of an unknown sailor from the *Mary Rose* (wrecked off Portsmouth in 1545) has added a further poignant maritime focus, this time inside the cathedral in the Navy Aisle. The cathedral began as the parish church of St Thomas of Canterbury, and became a cathedral in 1927 with the creation of the new diocese of Portsmouth.

The east end is the earliest part of the building, now the chapel of St Thomas, with a splendid hanging pyx by Hector Miller. The chancel was completed in the Transitional style in 1185 – the dedication to Thomas Becket was topical, since he had been martyred in Canterbury Cathedral in 1170. The original medieval church continued westward to form a cruciform building with a tower at its west end. The core of this building is still clearly seen in the transepts (now the Lady Chapel, and the Chapel of Healing and Atonement) and in the shape of the central part of the choir (the original nave).

During the Civil War the church was bombarded from Gosport by Parliamentary troops and severe damage was sustained. The nave and tower were left ruinous and this led to the deterioration of the fine medieval wall-painting, some of which is still preserved in the north transept. By 1691, the nave and tower were rebuilt in the restrained elegance of the William and Mary Classical style. Already Gothic and Classic stood side by side.

The foundation of the new diocese of Portsmouth brought another architectural style into play. Sir Charles Nicholson added tower transepts and the beginnings of a nave in Rhenish Romanesque. By 1939 these plans had been completed as far as the third bay of the nave. The completion of the cathedral had to wait until 1991, although Michael Drury's final bay and west end do reflect Nicholson's vision. Included are a Byzantine-style font beneath the tower and the new bronze west doors, representing the tree of life, which were designed by Bryan Kneale and were dedicated in 1998. The original Golden Barque weathervane is now within the cathedral itself.

The choir and presbytery.

The fifteenth-century stone reredos.

WINCHESTER CATHEDRAL

The beginnings of Winchester Cathedral lie back in the seventh-century missions to England when St Birinus baptised King Cynegils of the West Saxons in the year 635. In 634 King Cenwalh built a minster at Winchester and Bishop Haeddi transferred his see there around three decades later, establishing the minster as his cathedral. Winchester thus became a royal and ecclesiastical centre – mortuary chests with the bones of early kings and queens are still in the possession of the cathedral; Alfred the Great, King of Wessex, was buried nearby in New Minster in 899. In the 960s Bishop Ethelwold re-founded the cathedral as a Benedictine priory, dedicated to St Swithun, the ninth-century saint. The replacement of the Saxon bishop Stigand with Walkelin, a Norman, in 1070 marks the beginnings of the present cathedral. Walkelin began building in 1079 and the first part of the building was dedicated in 1093. Most of the bishop's cathedral has been rebuilt and, above ground, only the transepts give us an idea of the appearance of his cathedral.

The modest but noble Perpendicular work on the west front gives way to the magnificent nave, also Perpendicular in style. The present nave is not as long as its Romanesque predecessor, but its majesty contributes to making Winchester the longest cathedral in England, at a total length of 169 metres (556 feet). The remodelling of the nave was begun by Bishop William Edington in the mid-fourteenth century and completed by the famous Bishop William of Wykeham, who was the founder of both New College, Oxford, and Winchester College. The nave's height and vaulting give it a splendid dignity. The two transepts are the only remaining examples of Romanesque work from Bishop Walkelin's time although the eleventh-century crypt also survives.

More Perpendicular arcading can be found in the nineteenth-century choir screen, while the choir itself is set beneath the enormous arches of the central tower. The very fine choir stalls with misericords, dating from around 1308, are believed to be the work of William Lyngwode, a Norfolk carpenter. The wooden vaulting of the presbytery is built to mirror the stone vaulting of the nave. At the eastern end of the presbytery, between the choir and the retro-choir, is the remarkable Great Screen which dates from the late fifteenth century, with its numerous niches containing a series of stone figures. The original figures were broken up at the Reformation, but many have since been recovered and are now displayed in the triforium gallery; the present figures date from the late nineteenth century.

The retro-choir was opened up to its present enormous size around 1200 in the Early English style to house the shrine of St Swithun; this work was begun by Bishop Godfrey de Lucy, whose austere tomb of Purbeck marble stands within this retro-choir. St Swithun's relics were translated to their final resting place near to the present memorial in 1476, but in 1538, at the Dissolution, the shrine was destroyed and the location of Swithun's bones is unknown. The Lady Chapel, which was part of this place of pilgrimage, was altered and re-vaulted around 1500.

Surrounding the retro-choir are magnificent chantry chapels to Cardinal Henry Beaufort and Bishops William Waynflete, Richard Fox and Stephen Gardiner. (There are also two fine chantries in the nave to William of Edington and William of Wykeham.) The chantry chapels in Winchester are celebrated examples of such chapels which were built so that daily masses could be said by the monks for the bishops commemorated within them. William Waynflete stands alongside William of Wykeham as a great founder and benefactor in English education; he was Provost of Eton and founded Magdalen College, Oxford. Stephen Gardiner was the last bishop of Winchester to pay allegiance to the Pope, surviving the Reformations of both Henry VIII and Edward VI before dying during the reign of Mary Tudor.

Winchester Cathedral has associations with the writers Izaak Walton and Jane Austen, both of whom are buried here. There are also a number of important contemporary art commissions, including Antony Gormley's sculpture *Sound II* in the crypt and Peter Eugene Ball's *Christus* in the north transept. In the retro-choir, and on the screen separating the feretory from the shrine, are a number of modern icons, in the Byzantine style, by Sergei Fyodorov. Winchester, following the example of Walter Hussey in Chichester, has re-established the tradition of the Church as a patron of the arts.

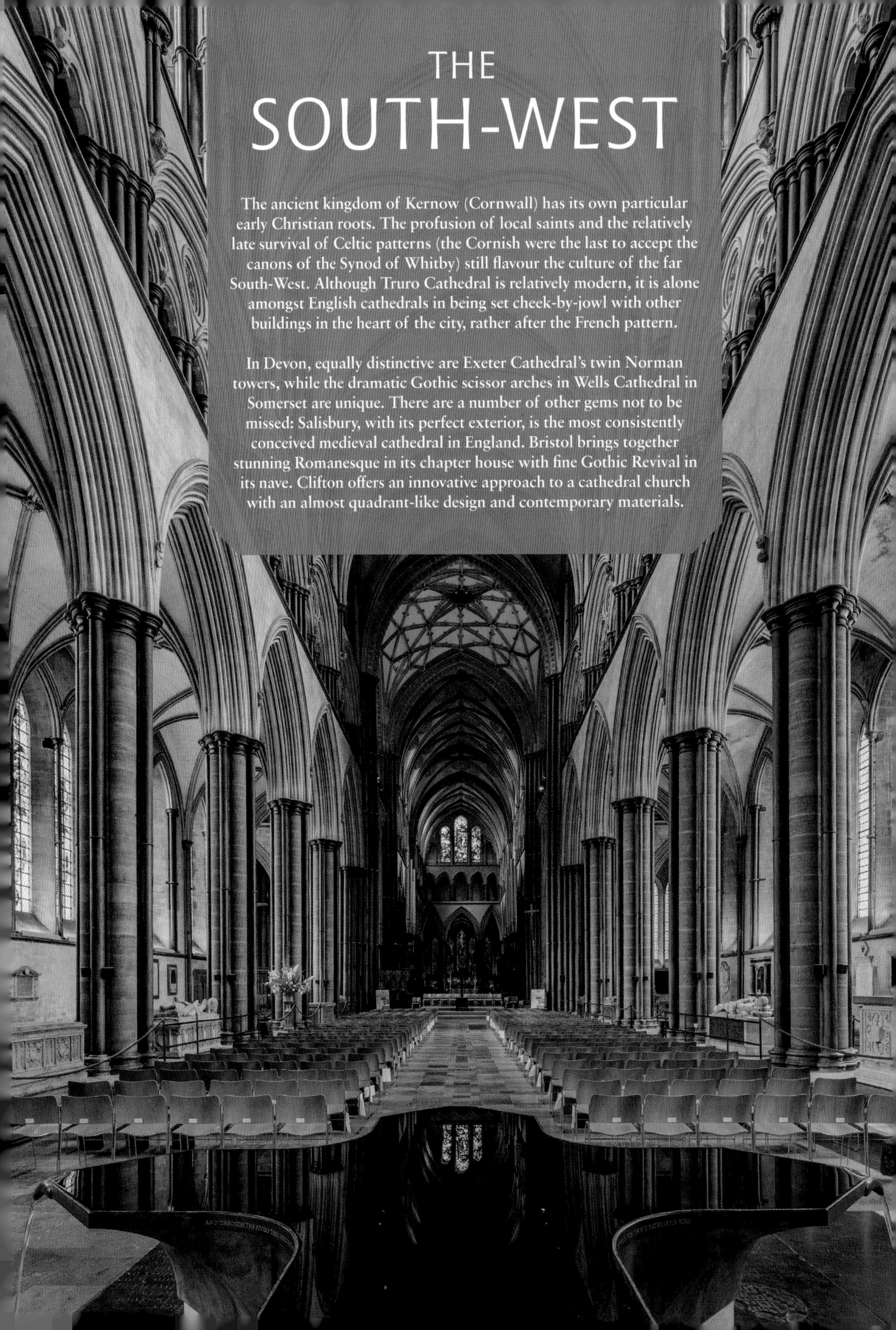

THE SOUTH-WEST

The ancient kingdom of Kernow (Cornwall) has its own particular early Christian roots. The profusion of local saints and the relatively late survival of Celtic patterns (the Cornish were the last to accept the canons of the Synod of Whitby) still flavour the culture of the far South-West. Although Truro Cathedral is relatively modern, it is alone amongst English cathedrals in being set cheek-by-jowl with other buildings in the heart of the city, rather after the French pattern.

In Devon, equally distinctive are Exeter Cathedral's twin Norman towers, while the dramatic Gothic scissor arches in Wells Cathedral in Somerset are unique. There are a number of other gems not to be missed: Salisbury, with its perfect exterior, is the most consistently conceived medieval cathedral in England. Bristol brings together stunning Romanesque in its chapter house with fine Gothic Revival in its nave. Clifton offers an innovative approach to a cathedral church with an almost quadrant-like design and contemporary materials.

BRISTOL CATHEDRAL

Bristol Cathedral is set on College Green at the centre of the city. It goes back to an initiative of Robert Fitzhardinge, who brought six Augustinian monks to establish the first abbey here in 1140. The first church, in Romanesque style, was probably completed in 1165. The chapter house, which leads off the eastern cloister walk, survives from the period, and is a particularly notable piece of Romanesque architecture. In 1220 the Elder Lady Chapel (the older of the two) was built in the new Gothic style. It is situated off the north transept, and it has exquisite carvings of foliage, beasts and human faces.

The choir is notable for the beautiful pattern made by the lierne ribs of the vaulting – among the earliest in England. The choir stalls contain some notable wood carving given by Abbot Elyot in about 1520 and they include some fine misericords.

The tower and transepts were re-fashioned in the period 1460–80 and the vaulting of the transepts and the crossing is particularly of note. When the abbey was closed by King Henry VIII in 1539, the monks had just embarked on a scheme to rebuild the nave in the Gothic style, the Romanesque nave having already been demolished in preparation for this. The cathedral remained without a nave until 1867, when G.E. Street began to build on the foundations of the original pillars.

J.L. Pearson, who designed Truro Cathedral, subsequently added the present high altar reredos and the choir screen. The western towers were completed in 1888, after Street's death.

Above: The choir looking west.
Opposite: Salisbury Cathedral.

SALISBURY CATHEDRAL

Like an intricate casket on a carpet of mown grass – this is but one description of the remarkable integrity of Salisbury Cathedral. This integrity and proportion, which we see uniquely in Salisbury, owes its origins to the initiative of Bishop Richard le Poore. In 1217, he petitioned the Pope for leave to remove his cathedral to a new site. The earlier cathedral had been built in Romanesque style by the Norman bishop Osmund. This cathedral had been at Old Sarum, and it was in this place, through the work of St Osmund, that the statutes of the cathedral were formulated and perhaps even during this period that the interest in liturgy, which gave birth to the 'Sarum Rite', began. As a site, however, Old Sarum was unsatisfactory – it was short of water and extremely exposed.

The new cathedral was begun in 1220 at a point where two rivers find their confluence with the Avon. The unity of its Early English architecture owes everything to the building being completed

The choir looking west.

Lady Chapel and Prisoners of Conscience window.

within 50 years. The masons started in the east with the Chapel of the Holy Trinity and All Saints; on its completion in 1225 it became the new site of the tomb of St Osmund, brought from Old Sarum. Despite Richard le Poore's move to Durham, the cathedral was still finished to the original design. The Trinity Chapel is the most daring and original part of the cathedral with its slender pillars of Purbeck marble and very narrow side aisles. The chapel was transfigured in 1980 with the addition of the magnificent Prisoners of Conscience window by Gabriel Loire of Chartres. Its use of thirteenth-century colouring and especially deep blue adds an aura of mystery to the whole cathedral with its wide and open vistas from west to east.

The building of the cathedral continued eastwards and the cloisters, too, were constructed in the period 1240–70. Salisbury was never a monastic foundation. The chapter house was completed between 1263 and 1284 and is a superb example of the Geometrical Decorated style with a roof fanning out from a single central pillar. The cathedral is built throughout from Jurassic limestone from Chilmark, to the west of Salisbury, while the pillars are of Purbeck marble from Worth Matravers, in Dorset. One of the merits of Salisbury Cathedral is the clarity and simplicity of its design. It is among the larger English cathedrals and its most majestic and famous feature is, of course, its spire. It is the tallest spire in England, reaching a height of 123 metres (404 feet). The construction of the spire is remarkable, being based upon an interior wooden scaffolding which remains to this day. The great load (6,400 tonnes) is borne by the four main central piers, supported by a series of internal stone buttresses, built into the thickness of the clerestory walls to help take the strain. Strainer arches were added in the fourteenth century at the entrance to the choir transepts, to supplement the other arches into the transept and to avoid the great piers collapsing inwards.

The bishop and chapter added a library over the eastern cloister in 1445. Within the library is a fine collection of medieval manuscripts, including a Gallican Psalter of the tenth century. Most famous of all is its copy of the Magna Carta. Originally this building was twice its present length and included the Chancellor's Lecture Room. The restoration of Salisbury Cathedral by James Wyatt from 1789 to 1792 has been much criticised, mainly because of what he removed, including the high altar, the thirteenth-century choir screen and the detached bell tower. He also took out the remaining thirteenth-century glass from the windows and removed two fifteenth-century chantry chapels; even so, the removal of these chapels restored the original plan of the cathedral. Thirty years later the high altar was replaced and the arrangement of the sanctuary reverted to the earlier plan.

Salisbury stands within the largest open close in England. Elizabeth Frink's sculpture, *Walking Madonna*, adds an interesting feature to the north-west corner of the Close, as the visitor approaches from the city gate. The city itself was begun at the same time as the cathedral and is the earliest example in England of a city built upon a planned 'grid' of streets. More recently the font by William Pye, with its flowing water, dramatically focuses baptism at the heart of Christian faith and worship.

WELLS CATHEDRAL

The elaborate and highly sculptured west front, the chapter house stairs and the great scissor arches at the crossing are more than sufficient reasons to make a special pilgrimage to Wells. That, combined with the springs that feed the moat of the Bishop's Palace, and give the city its name, offer something unparalleled in any English cathedral. The first church on this site was built by Aldhelm in 705; in 909 the diocese was founded, and Aldhelm's church became the cathedral. In 1088 it was rebuilt by Bishop Robert of Lewes, but not until 1244 did the Pope decree the diocese be named Bath and Wells, and the church became a cathedral once more.

Wells Cathedral was the first to be built wholly in English Gothic and much of the building is in Decorated style. The aisled nave dates from 1338–48. The crossing is dominated by William Joy's scissor arches, designed to bear the load of the tower, which was beginning to collapse under its own weight. The scissor arches exude both strength and grace. Beyond the pulpitum screen is the earliest part of the cathedral, begun around 1179. In 1320 the quire was extended eastwards, later connecting with the octagonal Lady Chapel which had been a quite separate building; there are fine stalls with misericords dating from the same period. There is good medieval glass in the east window and in the windows of the quire aisles. The Bulgarian Stations of the Cross are an interesting feature.

In the south transept is the Saxon font, the only surviving feature of the earlier church. Wells has always been governed by a dean and canons, and in early days was served by the Vicars Choral. To the east side of the north transept are the stunning

Above: The west front.

chapter house stairs, which lead eventually to the Chain Gate and Vicars' Hall, where the Vicars Choral meet. Although Wells was never a monastic foundation it has a particularly beautiful medieval cloister, which dates back to the fifteenth century.

In 1995 the Jerusalem Trust donated sculptures of the symbols of the four Evangelists, created by the Purbeck artist Mary Spencer-Watson. These substantial works in stone line the path to the north door of the cathedral. Newer developments include educational and Song School facilities completed in 2009.

The fourteenth-century scissor arches.

EXETER CATHEDRAL

While Christianity flowered in the seventh century through the work of Augustine and Theodore in the South-East, and Aidan and Cuthbert in Northumbria, other missionaries were having influence in the South-West. The most celebrated son of Devonshire at that time was St Boniface. Boniface became a key missionary to central Germany and his shrine can still be visited in the cathedral at Fulda. Willibald records that the young Boniface was educated in a monastery on the site of the present Exeter Cathedral. By petition of Pope Leo IX in 1050, Bishop Leofric transferred the see from Crediton to Exeter, and that marked the beginnings of both the diocese and the cathedral as we know it today.

Bishop Leofric had pre-empted the move that in most other cathedrals had to await the arrival of the Normans, and moved the see to an important commercial centre. The Normans, however, still left their mark. In 1107, William Warelwast, the nephew of William the Conqueror, became the bishop of Exeter. Warelwast built the Romanesque cathedral, including Exeter's celebrated twin Norman towers, which now form the transepts. This arrangement is unique in English cathedrals and is reflected in a similar pattern found in the parish church of Ottery St Mary, near Exeter, which was established by Bishop Grandisson as a foundation for a Vicars Choral on the model of the cathedral. Bishop Warelwast's cathedral was completed in 1133.

The cathedral seen today is the product of a remarkable succession of episcopates, covering in total more than 100 years. The first of these great building bishops was Walter Bronescombe. He arrived in Exeter in 1258. By the time of his death in

The west front.

The longest continuous vault of any English cathedral.

1280 the walls of the Lady Chapel reached to the window sills, and the abutting chapels of St Gabriel and St John the Evangelist were almost complete. Bronescombe was succeeded by Bishop Peter Quinel, whose first achievement was to convert the twin Norman towers into transepts, giving birth to the majestic arches. When Quinel died in 1291, the Lady Chapel was finished and he was buried in a tomb which stands before the altar in the chapel. The third bishop of significance in this work was Bishop Bytton, who built the four eastern bays of the choir. The throne, sedilia and the pulpitum screen that divides nave from choir were completed between 1308 and 1326 by Bishop Stapeldon, and the misericords come from this same period. The final bishop of this great quadrumvirate was John Grandisson, who was bishop for 42 years from 1327 to 1369. He built the nave with its 30 Purbeck marble pillars and its magnificent Gothic vaulting. There being no central tower, the vaulting continues from one end of the cathedral to the other, forming the longest unbroken stretch of Gothic vaulting in the world. The cathedral remains substantially the building finished by Grandisson. Part of his achievement is the splendid Minstrels' Gallery in the north triforium of the nave, which includes carvings of minstrels carrying fourteenth-century instruments.

Exeter is notable for its fine tombs and chantry chapels. Amongst these chantries is that founded by Sir John Speke in 1517 – one of the later architectural glories of the cathedral. The Reformation marked the ending of medieval patterns of prayer for the dead and the beginning of a different theological approach to death, and the chantry chapels are a reminder of that older tradition.

To the south of the cathedral are some surviving parts of the cloister. Exeter had a cloister even though it is an 'Old Foundation' cathedral whose life was ordered by a dean and canons rather than by a monastic community, as in the case of Winchester, Worcester and Norwich. Exeter suffered considerably from the ravages of both the Reformation and the Puritan Revolution; images were removed and defaced and the reredos was despoiled – happily this was restored (albeit badly) in 1638. During the Commonwealth a brick wall was built over the screen, effectively producing two churches, one used by the Independents (early Congregationalists) and the other by the Presbyterians. After the restoration of the monarchy, the wall was removed and much was done to restore the cathedral's beauty. More recently the cathedral suffered in the Second World War, with the windows and St James' Chapel damaged during aerial bombardment. Exeter Cathedral is now in a splendid state of conservation and it stands as a church of particular and unusual beauty within the South-West.

TRURO CATHEDRAL

Nowhere else in England are the early Celtic roots of Christianity so obvious as in the profusion of local saints in Cornwall. In contrast to this, however, John Loughborough Pearson's Cathedral Church of St Mary the Virgin, in Truro, has the distinction of being the first entirely new foundation since the Reformation. Pearson's vision was of a cathedral in the Anglo-French style tucked into the heart of the city, using the south aisle of the medieval parish church of St Mary as the outer south aisle of the new cathedral choir. The whole concept is Gothic Revival using a beautifully consistent Early English style. The stone is local – granite from Mabe for the exterior, and ashlar from St Stephens for the inside of the building, but the finer external detail is in Bath stone.

The nave of eight bays is relatively plain, but, as with all of Pearson's churches, it offers distant vistas into other parts of the building – the retro-choir, the transepts and the sanctuary in particular. Both nave and sanctuary have a modest triforium and a high clerestory – the height to the top of the vaulting is 21 metres (70 feet). The choir and transepts were built in seven years and completed in 1887. The consecration was performed by Edward White Benson, who had moved four years earlier from being the first bishop of Truro to become Archbishop of Canterbury. In the 20 years that followed, the nave and central tower, with its spire reaching 76 metres (250 feet), were completed. The two western towers were blessed in 1910.

The interior work encompasses some stunning detail. The elaborate and beautiful reredos is of Bath stone with a series of fine sculptures. The baptistry on the south side is a perfect study in Early English with clustered shafts and wall arcading built on shafts of Cornish serpentine. The font and its plinth are of a rose-coloured African marble. The windows of the cathedral form one of the finest collections of English nineteenth and early twentieth-century glass. The chapter house is in a modern idiom and was completed and dedicated in 1967. The building's position in the centre of this small Cornish city is unique among English cathedrals and is a powerful focus for the whole county.

Above: The three spires.

Truro Cathedral's crossing vault.

CLIFTON CATHEDRAL

The modern Roman Catholic Cathedral of St Peter and St Paul at Clifton in Bristol replaced the pro-cathedral dedicated to the Apostles, which opened finally in 1848. The new cathedral has benefited from the insights of the contemporary liturgical movement, hence the altar effectively stands at the focus of a quadrant, giving good sight lines for the congregation.

Externally, there is a striking *flèche* containing a cross and two bells. The construction is of shuttered concrete and the clarity of the main structure allows the internal furnishings to speak eloquently. The font of Portland Stone with a spangled Purbeck bowl is by Simon Verity; there is some fine lettering around the rim. The Stations of the Cross, the entrance doors and the ambo and lectern are by William Mitchell. The altar is square and also of Portland stone. The overall effect of the interior of the cathedral is one of striking simplicity.

The striking interior.

SCOTLAND

Scotland has played an important part in the evangelisation of Britain. As early as the fifth century, St Ninian had set up his Candida Casa or White House in Galloway. From here he would be a missionary to the southern Picts. Later, in the sixth century, Columba arrived from Derry in Ireland, in 563 establishing a monastery on Iona. In the seventh century, King Oswald would invite Aidan to come from Iona and set up a new monastery at Lindisfarne in Northumbria. Back in the fifth century, a wider network of monastic missionaries were at work in Scotland, including St Mungo (Kentigern) who is said to be the founder of the great cathedral in Glasgow.

The Reformation in Scotland wrought a heavy toll on the medieval churches and cathedrals of the nation. Although the broader process of Reformation was relatively peaceful, ecclesiastical buildings were generally left to decay and become ruinous.

The nineteenth and twentieth centuries have seen some revival, and the selection of buildings collected here attempts to offer examples of cathedrals from the earliest period and up to the twentieth century within the Presbyterian, Episcopalian and Roman Catholic traditions.

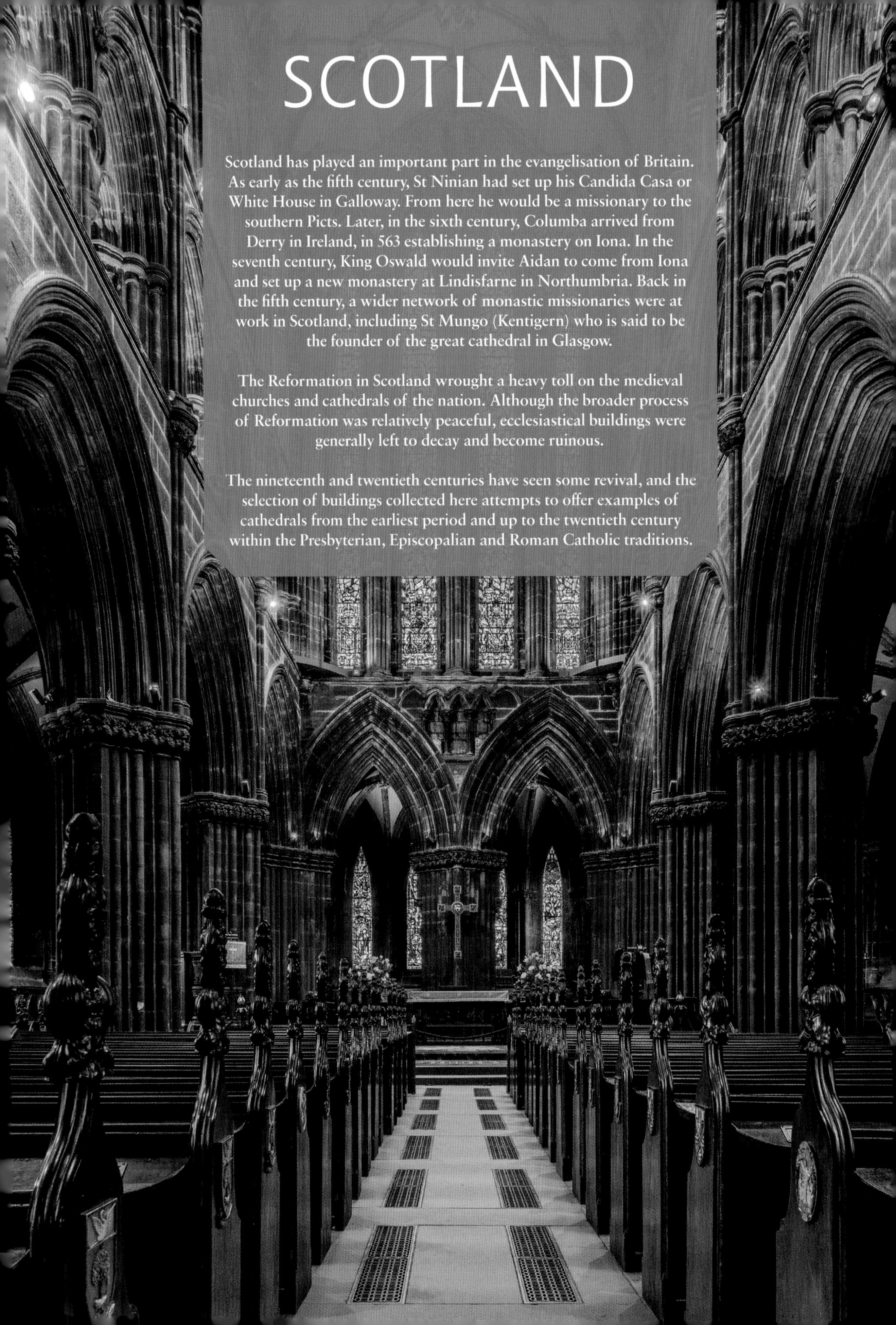

CATHEDRAL OF ST MAGNUS, KIRKWALL

Although no real distance from the Scottish coast, the Orkney Islands did not become part of Scotland until the late fifteenth century – 1468 to be precise. The background, the history and the names are almost entirely Norse in origin. This makes sense of the construction of the magnificent cathedral of St Magnus in this northern outpost of Britain.

The story of Magnus is told in the *Orkneyinga Saga* and it relates to the division of the islands into two fiefdoms headed at the time by two earls, Magnus and Haakon. The feud between these two cousins reached a climax in 1117 when an attempted reconciliation was planned. Haakon, however, brought a great military force. In the ensuing encounter, Magnus, the more peaceable of the two cousins, was murdered. His reputation for holiness spread far and wide. Magnus' nephew Rognvald came from Norway and in 1129 overthrew Haakon's son. He vowed to build a stone church dedicated to his murdered uncle.

Building began in 1137 and ultimately both Magnus and Rognvald would be buried there – their tombs are in the wall of the choir. The core of the church is a strong Romanesque nave supported by blind arcading along the outer walls of the aisles of a most beautiful interleaved pattern; this blind arcading is there to support the great weight of the building. The crossing, transepts and two thirds of the nave were all in place by the 1150s. Twenty years later the crossing collapsed and the rebuilding included the construction of the unusual square chapels which mirror those in the great Norwegian cathedral at Nidaros (Trondheim); it seems most likely that some of the same masons were involved in the construction of both cathedrals, having come from Durham and then moving on to Nidaros after Orkney. The tower was completed in the fourteenth century and the bells date from 1528.

Twentieth-century conservation has added much to the cathedral. In 1919, during conservation work, the relics of St Magnus were found and restored to their place in the cathedral. Much of the excellent wooden furnishing from the twentieth century is the work of George Mackie Watson. In 1965, the most easterly part of the church was dedicated to St Rognvald. A fine sculpted wooden figure of St Magnus was the gift of the Bishop of Nidaros for the cathedral's 800th anniversary in 1937.

Above: St Magnus' Romanesque nave.
Opposite: Glasgow Cathedral.

ST MACHAR'S, ABERDEEN

St Machar, to whom Aberdeen's ancient cathedral is dedicated, is believed to have been an Irish missionary to the Picts working in the area which is now Aberdeen. The cathedral was established in 1165 and is deceptive in its appearance. Approached by a fine avenue, the massing of the distinctive and powerful west front with its twin towers, capped with short spires, gives the cathedral its nobility.

The episcopate of Henry le Cheyne (1282–1329) heralded the building of the new church. The choir was finished in the reign of Robert I (the Bruce), following his victory at Bannockburn. Alexander de Kininmund (1355–80) built the nave. William Elphinstone (1483–1514) added a central tower and a new choir – both modelled on St John's Church in Perth. With Gavin Dunbar came the fine decorated ceiling and the western spires, with Thomas French completing the transepts in 1530.

Only the nave and western towers survive complete. The central tower collapsed in 1688, bringing down the choir and transepts with it. The nave roof, after its lead had been stripped off just after the Reformation in 1568, was renewed in 1607. In 1832 restoration began and continued throughout the nineteenth century.

The west front, the cathedral's great glory, is of pink granite. Set in the centre of the west front are seven slender windows. Another great glory of the cathedral is Bishop Dunbar's square panelled ceiling. The panels have diagonal ribs surmounted with heraldic shields.

The nave and heraldic ceiling.

ST COLUMBA'S CATHEDRAL, OBAN

Returning by ferry from Mull into Oban, the tower of St Columba's Roman Catholic Cathedral is the commanding feature of the skyline. Built between 1930 and 1953, St Columba's is a classic example of the strength and originality of Giles Gilbert Scott's work. Grandson of Sir Gilbert Scott, Giles was also the architect of the Anglican cathedral in Liverpool.

This great church replaces a corrugated iron building erected in 1886 with help from the Marquess of Bute, and known throughout its relatively brief existence as 'the tin cathedral'. Scott's building is constructed from snecked Aberdeenshire granite and breathes a sense of space, majesty and austerity throughout. It gains its atmosphere of transcendence through this grandeur rather than through manifold architectural detail. The simplicity of the building is enhanced by the use of lancets, not only those grouped together in the fenestration of the aisles, but also in the great south western tower.

The interior gains further presence with the use of different granites, the absence of a clerestory, and in the timber used in two of the reredos. Looking out toward Mull and the more distant Iona, the cathedral is both a noble and powerful symbol of Columba, who, in the sixth century, brought Christianity back to Scotland, and through Aidan and others, to England.

Viewed from McCaig's Tower.

ST NINIAN'S CATHEDRAL, PERTH

Perth's history can be traced back at least as far as 1120 when a motte castle was already part of the landscape. From 1150, it became the seat of the Sheriff and its importance grew as a nodal centre, at the crossing of the Tay. The history of St Ninian's Cathedral is much more recent; it was the first new cathedral built in Britain since the Reformation. It came about at the initiative of two Anglo-Catholic Episcopalian laymen: its establishment was a deliberately assertive act, intent on marking out the Scottish Episcopalian Church as the 'Catholic Church of the nation'.

When commissioned in 1848, William Butterfield, an enthusiastic Anglo-Catholic architect, faced a challenge. The site was not easy and finance was an issue. His initial design was for a four-bay nave, two western towers, transepts and a chancel of two long bays. The Butterfield design was built in two phases in 1850 and 1890. In 1899–1901 Frank Loughborough Pearson took up the mantle, rebuilding the chancel's north aisle with two broad and gracious arcades. Only one western tower was built, by Pearson to a modified Butterfield design.

The interior is of an impressive height and Ninian Comper's superb rood beam adds majesty. The roofs were restored in the extensive 2017 restoration. In 1936, the architectural partnership of Tarbolton and Ochterlony extended the cloister and built an adjoining school. The cathedral has a varied collection of fine stained glass.

The east end.

DUNBLANE CATHEDRAL

The nave and ribbed wagon ceiling.

This is one of the most impressive surviving buildings from medieval Scotland partly on account of its sheer size, but partly due also to the significant restorations of the nineteenth century.

The first mention we have of a bishop in Dunblane is in 1155, although it is likely that by then the see was already well established. The next significant and dramatic episode in the cathedral's history came with the Reformation in 1559–60, after which the nave was roofless and remained so for 300 years. In the late nineteenth century, architect Robert Rowand Anderson embarked upon a radical and far-reaching restoration bringing the ruined nave back into use.

The interior of the nave echoes a rare dignity and nobility, and Anderson's modern ribbed wagon ceiling is a clear success; the choir screen and communion table are also by Anderson. Sir Robert Lorimer was responsible for the handsome nave pews, the choir stalls and the organ case – all part of the 1912–14 additions. The vaulting in the Chapter House is another fine feature of this splendid cathedral, one of Scotland's greatest survivals from the Middle Ages. In the south aisle there is a stone commemorating the children killed in the Dunblane school tragedy in 1996.

ST GILES' HIGH KIRK, EDINBURGH

Starting from the bottom of the High Street, and climbing up the Royal Mile, there are perhaps four key landmarks: the Palace of Holyroodhouse sets us on our way and just a little way up, the Tolbooth reaches out on the right; soon after this the Castle, at the far end, becomes visible. Before we reach there, however, on the left is St Giles' High Kirk with its unmistakeable crown steeple. Strictly speaking, as one can see from the entry in this book on St Mary's Episcopal Cathedral, St Giles was only a cathedral for two brief periods: 1633–38 and 1663–89. However, it is effectively the grandest of all the Scottish great burgh churches. It is often said to project four different personalities – a medieval burgh church, a late Georgian exterior, a somewhat gloomy Victorian interior and a Post-Reformation preaching box with four sub-divisions. The present building is more than the sum of these parts.

The burgh was founded in 1130 and St Giles was born soon after, even though now the only evidence we have of the twelfth century is one scalloped capital. The church was entirely rebuilt in the 200-year period immediately before the Reformation. Exactly as we see the building now with regard to length, a nave of five bays was completed by 1387 with the choir being finished in 1419. In 1453 further building began, and in 1467 the two eastern bays of the choir were rebuilt with a clerestory and in a more lavish style. The lower stages of the tower date from *c.* 1400 with the crown steeple being completed in 1474; it was almost certainly modelled on the spire of St Nicholas' Cathedral in Newcastle-upon-Tyne – itself based on the spire of St Mary-le-Bow in London, which was later demolished. St Giles' central tower and steeple were heightened just before 1500.

In 1560, all the medieval screens were destroyed

The distinctive crown spire.

The reordered nave.

and the three western bays were taken as an annexe to the Tolbooth. Then, in 1581, the building was divided into three churches – the divisions came down in 1633, were restored again in 1639, and finally, all sub-divisions were abolished in 1882. In his 1833 restoration, the architect William Burn formally made the building into three churches and, at the same time he restored the exterior. The clearance of the streets surrounding the exterior had begun earlier, in 1817. The nave clerestory and plaster vault are the work of William Burn, but Burn's west doorway was itself replaced by the fine work of William Hay in 1881. The choir is arguably the best piece of late medieval architecture in Scotland. St Giles' is effectively a 'hall' type church like many of the Hanseatic city churches in Northern Europe, with the nave aisles reaching to the same height as the choir itself.

St Giles' is a complex building with numerous chapels and aisles. The late nineteenth-century Chapel of Youth lies in the north aisle, with the Preston Aisle south of the south choir. From this opens out the Chepman Aisle, named after the first Scottish printer. St John's Chapel is clearly Perpendicular in style, but the crossing may date back to 1387, although the capitals, bases and arches are later and from the fifteenth century.

ST MARY'S CATHEDRAL, EDINBURGH

Gilbert Scott's three spires command one's view of the western end of Robert Adam's Edinburgh 'New Town'. They were an unexpected gift to the horizon of Scotland's capital. Indeed, for 250 years, after the Glorious Revolution of 1688 there was no cathedral. It was not until Barbara and Mary Walker, heirs to Sir Patrick Walker of Easter Coates, gave their house and land for the building of a cathedral that St Mary's would become a reality. After a competition, won by Sir Gilbert Scott, the new church was begun. The main structure was completed by 1879, with the Chapter House built in 1890–91 to designs of Scott's son, John Oldrid Scott. The western spires were completed between 1913 and 1917. Scott left the next door Easter Coates house alone, but in 1903 the building was remodelled and became St Mary's Music School.

The central spire of the cathedral is only a little short of 91 metres (300 feet) high, with the western spires almost 70 metres (200 feet) to their tips. Scott's building picks up themes and designs from a number of places. The west doorway pays tribute to Holyrood, whose land this once had been; blind arches and gablets reflect Dunblane and Elgin; the rose window in the south transept echoes Lincoln.

The pulpit and King Charles' Chapel on the north side are by Oldrid Scott; the fine wrought iron screen is by Francis Skidmore of Coventry, designer of the famous choir screen in Hereford Cathedral. The Resurrection Chapel by Sir Robert Lorimer was dedicated in 1922 and is now a war memorial for the dead of both World Wars. In this transept too is the striking Millennium Window, designed by Sir Eduardo Paolozzi. The Rood Cross is also by Lorimer and again is part of the war memorial.

One cannot leave St Mary's without reference to the two celebrated paintings by A.E. Borthwick, entitled *The Presence*. Both the light in the distance and the figure of light next to the kneeling penitent represent Christ's presence in the Eucharist and in the prayers of the faithful.

The nave looking east.

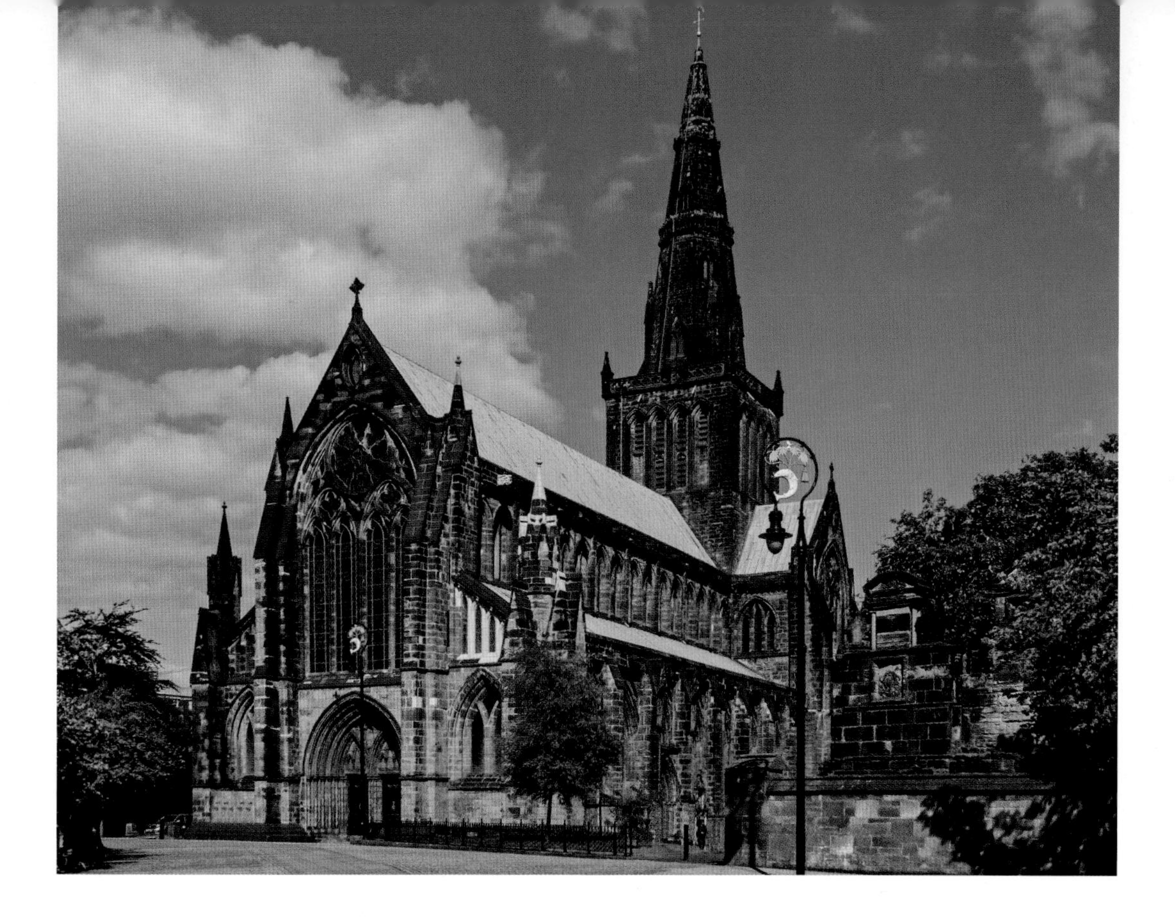

GLASGOW CATHEDRAL

Glasgow Cathedral's position, fairly high on the hillside at Townhead, to the north east of the main city centre is not unusual amongst Scottish cities; the sacred centre is rather apart from the commercial heart. Its present setting, however, is entirely different from the pivotal place it would have had in the Middle Ages. Eighteenth and nineteenth-century rebuilding and the clearance of cottages and other buildings in the 1960s, have given it a further idiosyncratic ambience, standing today amidst contemporary residential buildings for the University of Strathclyde. Its other most immediate neighbours are the Infirmary, the splendid Victorian necropolis and most recently the rather mixed baronial and modern style of the visitor centre. Nonetheless, this triumphant church, a unique survivor of its period in Scotland, remains a key cultural and religious landmark.

The origins of the cathedral lie in the sixth century with the legends surrounding St Kentigern (more often known by his nickname St Mungo). Of Kentigern, we have no certain history: his death, in 612, is mentioned in the *Annales Cambriae*. Kentigern is believed to have established a monastery on this site which then would also become the site of his cathedral. A historical silence follows and we only have reliable evidence of a succession of bishops from the mid-eleventh century onwards. Thereafter the cathedral was also deemed to be the place of the saint's relics.

We know that during the reign of King David I of Scotland, the king's former tutor, John, was appointed bishop. Bishop and king battled, unsuccessfully at the time, to establish a diocese independent of the Archbishop of York. Bishop John's building was part of this process and it was consecrated in 1136; excavations carried out in 1992 located what may have been the cathedral's west front – none of John's relatively modest cathedral remains visible. The next significant builder was Bishop Jocelin, who began enlarging the church in the early 1180s; despite a fire during the construction, the new cathedral was complete and consecrated in 1197.

From 1233 to 1258, Bishop William Bondington would construct a two-level extension to the east,

Above: Viewed from Cathedral Square.

The nave looking west.

being the choir with a crypt beneath. Transepts followed the choir in 1277 and the nave was completed soon after. There was doubtless some delay on account of war with England (Bishop Robert Wishart was accused of building siege engines from timber destined for the cathedral). This was the period of King Edward I (the 'hammer of the Scots') of England's brutal assault on Scotland. Despite his aggressive campaign, Edward still found time to stop as a pilgrim and make offerings at the shrine of Kentigern.

Bishop John Cameron (1426–46) was responsible for the building of the stone spire, with the double-storeyed Chapter House being completed soon after by Bishop William Turnbull (1447–54). The last important medieval addition was the Bishop Blacader Aisle built *c.* 1500 and intended originally as an undercroft to a building of full height.

The beginnings of the Scottish Reformation in 1560 spelt a very different future for the cathedral. By 1635, the choir had been walled off and, in 1647, the five western bays were similarly walled in; galleries were constructed over the aisles. Finally, in the first of the nineteenth-century restorations, the two western towers were demolished. The intention had been to replace them, but this never happened.

Despite the rather mixed building history, there can be seen clearly today a real homogeneity of late thirteenth-century Gothic. At the time there was still much contact with northern England, although the cathedral is not overly dependent on the architectural styles of its southern neighbour. The original rectangular plan has survived alongside the random later additions. The nobility of the three storey nave was restored as nineteenth-century work removed the internal walls.

The fine early fourteenth-century pulpitum leads into the choir where the stepped massing offers one of the most remarkable and unusual features of the building through the extra height produced. The eastern windows are enclosed in four tall slender lancets. They are set above the unusual double arcade affording views of what may have been a later site for the shrine of Kentigern.

The crypt so enclosed by this stepping was the original repository of St Mungo's relics and thus his shrine. In the south west crypt survives a small fragment of wall from Jocelin's church; it comprises a vertical shaft engaged with the wall and with delicate and beautiful carving in the capital. A miniature arcade in the south-east chapel is most likely a fragment of the base of Kentigern's shrine; nearby is St Kentigern's Well, from which water is still drawn for liturgical purposes. The cathedral contains a rich variety of stained glass from a number of periods, including rare Munich glass high up in the transepts, and some fine twentieth-century glass in the east window, the nave and the Blacader Aisle.

CATHEDRAL OF THE ISLES

Just two miles off the coast of Ayrshire at Largs lies Great Cumbrae, Scotland's most accessible island. The outstanding building of Millport, Cumbrae's only substantial settlement, is the Cathedral of the Isles. This architectural gem, deliberately built in the relative isolation of an island setting, was effectively an experiment born of the Oxford Movement, the movement which aimed to bring Anglicanism closer to its roots in the western catholic tradition.

The initiative to build came from George Boyle, who later became the sixth Earl of Glasgow and was strongly supported in the venture by John Keble, one of the founders of the Oxford Movement. Set up first of all as a 'collegiate church' it was completed in 1851 according to the designs of William Butterfield, one of the outstanding Anglo-Catholic architects of the nineteenth century; Butterfield was known for his adventurous use of colour and innovative design.

The smallest cathedral in Britain, it nevertheless displays extraordinary quality in miniature. Part of the original vision was the neighbouring College of the Holy Trinity which grows out of the cathedral itself and was founded to train clergy for Gaelic ministry. The entrance to the church is through the striking south west tower which leads into a deliberately dark and plain nave; the nave represents the earth. The roof is of simple pitched construction and the floor has encaustic tiles which are a feature of the building. Entering the chancel takes one into heaven: the ceiling depicts the islands' ferns and wild flowers and the walls again feature encaustic tiles; here there is colour all around.

Butterfield's polychrome inventiveness is particularly in evidence in the chancel. There is a Lady Chapel to the north east of the chancel. In the grounds of the cathedral, there is a 'wheel cross' commemorating George Boyle whose faith inspired the building.

The spire, the cathedral and ancillary buildings.

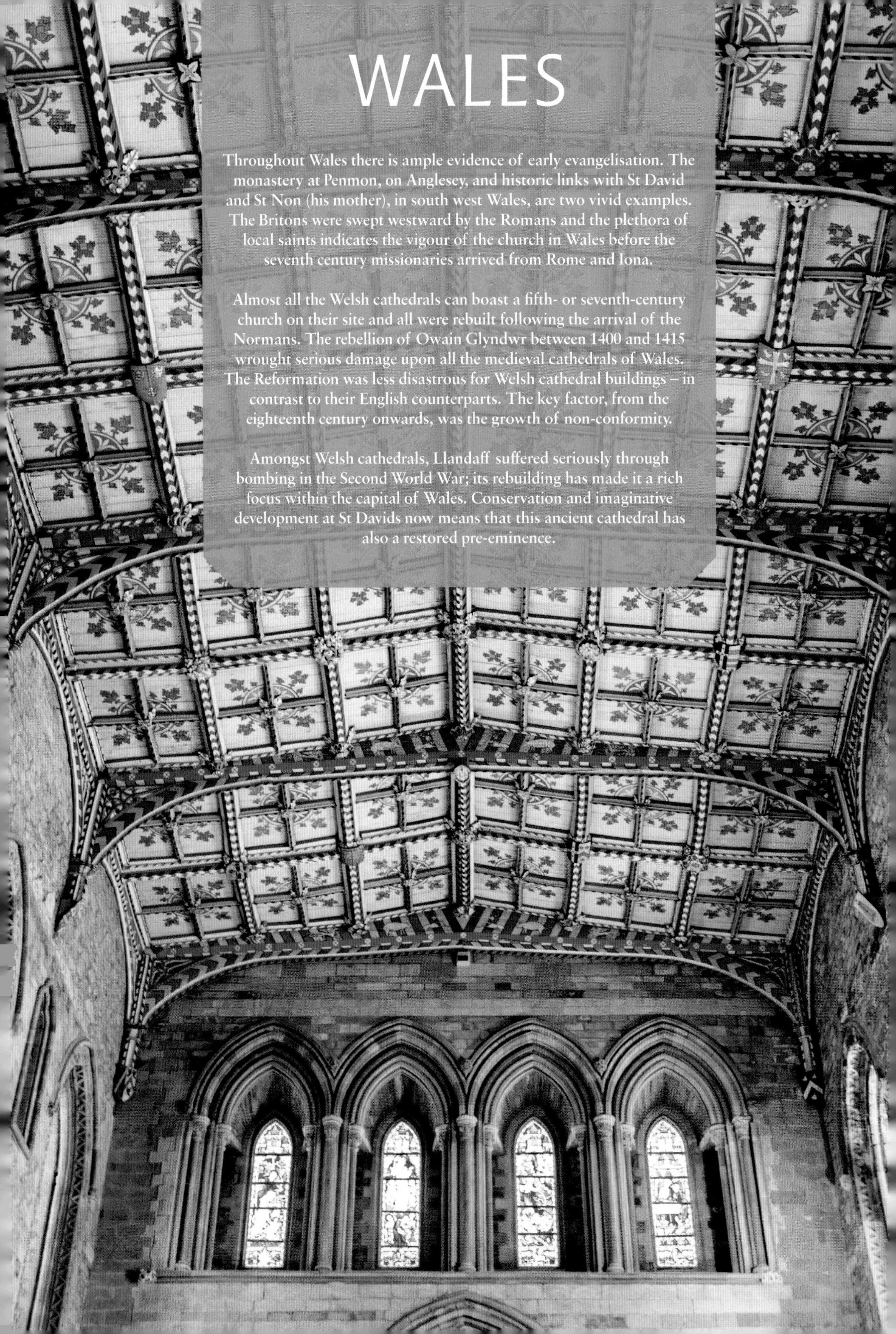

WALES

Throughout Wales there is ample evidence of early evangelisation. The monastery at Penmon, on Anglesey, and historic links with St David and St Non (his mother), in south west Wales, are two vivid examples. The Britons were swept westward by the Romans and the plethora of local saints indicates the vigour of the church in Wales before the seventh century missionaries arrived from Rome and Iona.

Almost all the Welsh cathedrals can boast a fifth- or seventh-century church on their site and all were rebuilt following the arrival of the Normans. The rebellion of Owain Glyndwr between 1400 and 1415 wrought serious damage upon all the medieval cathedrals of Wales. The Reformation was less disastrous for Welsh cathedral buildings – in contrast to their English counterparts. The key factor, from the eighteenth century onwards, was the growth of non-conformity.

Amongst Welsh cathedrals, Llandaff suffered seriously through bombing in the Second World War; its rebuilding has made it a rich focus within the capital of Wales. Conservation and imaginative development at St Davids now means that this ancient cathedral has also a restored pre-eminence.

ST ASAPH CATHEDRAL

St Asaph, deemed to be the second smallest city in Britain (only just behind St Davids), has had an exciting history in which the cathedral has played a significant part. Its history begins with a cross-Celtic connection. St Mungo (St Kentigern) was expelled from his own diocese of Glasgow and, fleeing to north Wales, he founded this new diocese in *c.* 560. Following St Mungo's return to his Scottish see, St Asaph, from whom the see would take its name, succeeded him as bishop here. The cathedral was re-founded in 1143, as part of the wider Norman reorganisation of the Welsh church; St Asaph was the last of the four ancient dioceses to be established.

Although it is often labelled as the smallest cathedral in England and Wales, none other than Dr Johnson commented that it has 'something of dignity and grandeur' about it. The cruciform building was begun in 1239 with the choir originally being Early English in style; indeed, that style only disappeared in the remodelling of the eighteenth century. In 1282, Edward I burnt the cathedral as retribution for Bishop Anian II's suspected complicity with a local rebellion. The cathedral was effectively completed in 1391–92 with the construction of the central tower by Robert Fagan of Chester.

The cathedral was not left in peace for long, however, for it was burnt again in 1402 in the rebellion of Owain Glyndwr. Those tempestuous times are reflected in the 'uncapitalised' nave arcading – the work of masons who must have been mostly engaged in military construction.

The eighteenth-century remodelling of the choir was by Joseph Turner, and the rigorous nineteenth-century restoration by Sir Gilbert Scott, who, unusually for Scott, replaced Turner's vaulting with timber work. The choir is almost entirely his work and features some first-class furnishings, including the lectern and the canopied episcopal throne or cathedra. The stalls, which have oscillated over the centuries between choir and crossing, are originally from the late fifteenth century.

Excitement in the cathedral continued even into the twentieth century. In 1930 and again in 1935, John Oldrid Scott, a son of Sir Gilbert, was called in to stabilise the tower, believed to be showing evidence of subsidence on account of an underground stream.

Opposite: St Davids Cathedral.
Below: St Asaph's choir with timber ceiling.

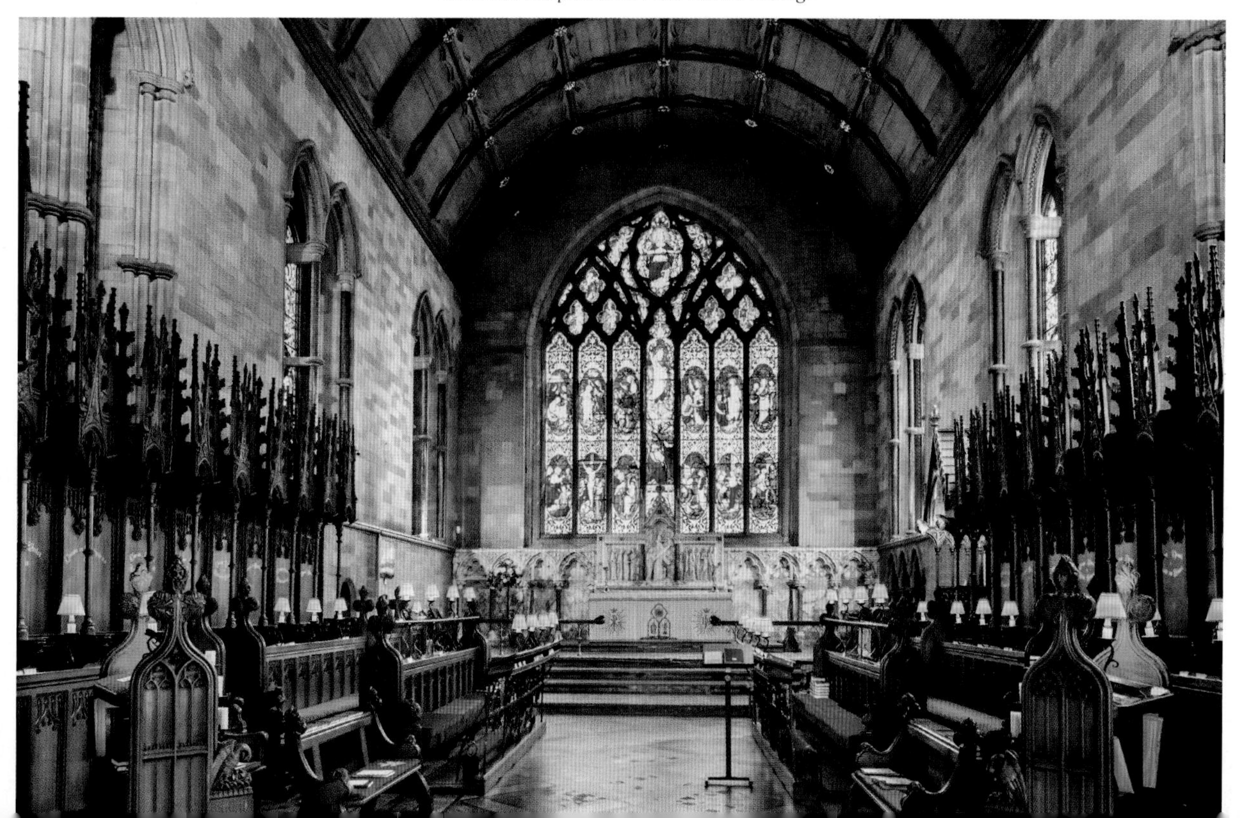

BANGOR CATHEDRAL

Sir Gilbert Scott's central tower.

Standing on the edge of the Menai Strait, Bangor is in a nodal position, set on an ancient site. St Deiniol completed his first monastic cell in 525 and he built on a low-lying site to avoid Viking raids. Nonetheless, it was still sacked in 634 and again in 1073.

The 'rebirth' of the cathedral came with the joint work of Gruffudd ap Cynan, King of Gwynedd and Bishop David, between 1120 and 1139. During this period, a cruciform church 40 metres (130 feet) in length was built, and consecrated in 1130. Less than 30 years after this, the cathedral was destroyed by King John's army, and so the later thirteenth century saw yet more rebuilding. The apse was replaced by an extended choir and, between 1285 and 1300, the transepts, along with the nave, were completed by Bishop Anian. The central tower was built in 1309, following further damage wrought by Edward I in 1282.

The next significant period of construction began in 1480. The present arcades and clerestory date from 1510, and the completion of the western tower marked the finishing of the renewed building.

The present cathedral, however, owes most to the radical restoration by Sir Gilbert Scott. Beginning in 1868, Scott was the architect of the central tower. This tower was further raised in height, with its pyramidal cap in 1969. One of the glories of the cathedral is the Mostyn Christ, a 'bound rood' with Christ seated on a rock, before his crucifixion; this dates from the fifteenth century and is fashioned from oak.

NEWPORT CATHEDRAL

Newport is the third city of Wales, and the site of the present cathedral of St Woolos is amongst the earliest of all Welsh cathedral sites. Beginning as a wooden church as early as *c.* 500, it was replaced by a stone building in the ninth century.

Following the growth of Norman hegemony in Wales, the ruinous building was replaced by a new one, to the east of the Saxon ruins. Its fine Romanesque core survives in the nave arcading and the outstanding western doorway, which is now an internal arch connecting the Lady Chapel and nave; the two tapering pillars on either side of the arch are believed to be Roman.

The impact of the Reformation was slower in this part of Wales. The church was eventually reordered as a preaching house with box pews. By the beginning of the nineteenth century, St Woolos had the appearance of a non-conformist chapel. During the nineteenth century three separate restorations gave the cathedral its present appearance. Twentieth-century alterations between 1960 and 1963 brought a new east end and choir by W.D. Caroe and an imaginative east window by John Piper.

St Woolos became temporary cathedral of the newly formed diocese of Monmouth in 1929 and in 1949 it was formally declared the cathedral.

The Norman archway.

BRECON CATHEDRAL

Placed on a ridge above the River Honddu, this dignified and noble church was an inspired choice to become the cathedral of the newly established diocese of Swansea and Brecon in 1923.

It was Bernard of Newmarch who established a Norman castle and priory here in Brecon, following his victory over Welsh leaders in 1093. He gave the church of 'St John the Evangelist without the walls' to his confessor, Roger, a monk of the Benedictine abbey at Battle in Sussex – the site of the Battle of Hastings. The font, the oldest object in the building with its grotesque masks (badly scarred – perhaps at the time of the Dissolution) would have had its place in the Norman church.

So, the church began as a Benedictine priory and it was the focus of prayers for local men leaving to fight for Henry V at Agincourt. At the Dissolution of the Monasteries in 1538, it became the parish church. Despite the disappearance of the monastic community, the claustral buildings largely survived: even the cloister itself remained partially intact until the eighteenth century. The original twelfth-century priory church was built from about 1230 onwards, and the architecture of the presbytery is an outstanding example of Early English work. Almost certainly, the masons responsible for Hereford Cathedral will have worked on the refurbishing. Building began (as was frequently the case) from the east end and the Early English style continues into the crossing and transepts. Construction resumed after a turbulent period, late in the thirteenth century and the climax of the work on the interior was reached with the Golden Rood in the fifteenth century. So remarkable was this rood, with its four orders or storeys, that the church became known as the Church of the Holy Rood – until the rood and screen were destroyed at the Dissolution.

Much restoration took place in the 1860s and 1870s, supervised largely by Sir George Gilbert Scott. Scott's work at Brecon enhanced the dignity and power of the building in many areas, and notably in his courageous completion of the stone vaulting in the presbytery. Further good work continued into the twentieth century with the rebuilding of St Lawrence's Chapel by W.D. Caroe in 1929–30; Caroe had earlier restored the powerful central tower in 1914. Sir Charles Nicholson restored the Havard Chapel, to honour a famous Welsh infantry regiment, in 1923. The Chapel of St Keyne in the north aisle became the Chapel of the Corvizons (Shoemakers), following the Dissolution.

Much of the priory complex survives, and has been well converted, including the Deanery and the Canonry, originally the Priory House. The tithe barn is now used as the Heritage Centre.

The tower and north transept.

ST DAVIDS CATHEDRAL

St Davids, Britain's smallest city, is set on the River Alun and perched on a rugged peninsula amongst some of the most stunning scenery in south-west Wales. Here, David, Abbot of Menevia, founded a cathedral in the mid-sixth century; he died in 589. David was the son of a pious mother, Non, who is remembered at Altarnun in Cornwall and indeed at her shrine and holy well, on the edge of St Davids. In the following four centuries, Vikings raided and pillaged the peninsular and at least two bishops, Moregenau and Abraham died; the stone marking Abraham's grave survives with its interesting Celtic inscriptions. It is now in Porth y Twr, the only remaining gatehouse to the cathedral precinct, where both the cathedral bells and an interpretation Centre now reside.

Following a pattern encountered across the land, the Normans re-founded the cathedral, and King Henry I appointed Bishop Bernard to the see. Bernard's new cathedral was consecrated in 1131. The most conspicuous early work now is the magnificent five-bay Romanesque nave. St Davids gained prestige when Pope Callixtus declared the saint's shrine to be a centre of pilgrimage for western Christianity. Henry II visited St Davids in 1181, from which time onwards further rebuilding began in order to enlarge the cathedral for pilgrims and others. All, however, was not to be plain sailing: the new tower collapsed in 1220 and earthquakes followed in 1247 and 1248.

It was Bishop Gower who was the inspiration

Above: Viewed from the gatehouse.

behind significant reconstruction from 1328 to 1347. The remarkable stone screen which marks out the cathedral as a two-roomed building, was Gower's work, as was the cathedra and heightened tower. In 1365 Bishop Adam Haughton, with the encouragement of John of Gaunt, began building St Mary's College and the cloister which connects the college to the cathedral. Bishop Edward Vaughan was responsible for the Holy Trinity Chapel, with its splendid fan vaulting; some believe this to have been executed by the same stone mason who worked on the roof of King's College, Cambridge. The nave has a sixteenth century oak roof.

The Reformation and Dissolution of the Monasteries wreaked havoc: Bishop Barlow allowed or even encouraged the desecration of David's shrine. Also in that period, Edmund Tudor's remains were translated from Carmarthen to the Holy Trinity Chapel. Edmund was the father of Henry VII and carried the title of the Earl of Richmond.

In the late eighteenth century, John Nash, the architect of the Prince Regent's London, completed some ineffective restoration. It was Sir Gilbert Scott, however, who – as elsewhere in Wales – effectively restored the building and saved it from ruin. He stabilised the tower and strengthened the rest of the building, re-created the Early English architectural style in the presbytery and added new furnishings.

The nave's sixteenth-century oak roof.

LLANDAFF CATHEDRAL

Discovering Llandaff is to encounter a surprisingly tranquil village surrounded on all sides by Cardiff's bustling metropolitan city centre. The 'village' itself is a treasure and the cathedral is a symbol of the survival of Christian faith throughout centuries of upheaval. The twelfth-century *Book of Llandaff* describes the tiny sixth-century cathedral as just 8.5 metres (28 feet) long and 4.5 metres (15 feet) wide. Following the arrival of the body of St Teilo in the sixth century, however, Llandaff became a place of pilgrimage. Teilo's place of burial survives, as do the tombs of two other local saints from the sixth and seventh centuries: Saints Dubricius and Oudoceus. The next clear date we have takes us all the way through to the twelfth century when the Normans installed Urban as the first Norman bishop of Llandaff in 1107; the arch into the Lady Chapel and the north door are both from Urban's era.

It was in 1120 that the Norman rebuilding began and the body of St Dyfrig was brought from Bardsey Island, site of an ancient monastery, just off the Pembrokeshire coast. With further work in 1170, the nave was broadened to its present width; the west front was completed in 1220. Both the present nave and the west front were commissioned by Henry of Abergavenny, bishop from 1193 to 1218. The cathedral was completed, including both the Lady Chapel and the Chapter House (built by Somerset masons using Chipping Camden and Bath stone), during the episcopate of William de Braose, who succeeded to the See of Llandaff in 1266. In 1400 the building was seriously damaged during the rebellion of Owain Glyndwr. After that damage had been repaired, further building followed and in 1485 the north-west tower was completed; the tower was the gift of Jasper Tudor, uncle of King Henry VII of England, who that year had succeeded to the throne

The cathedral stands on one of Britain's oldest Christian sites.

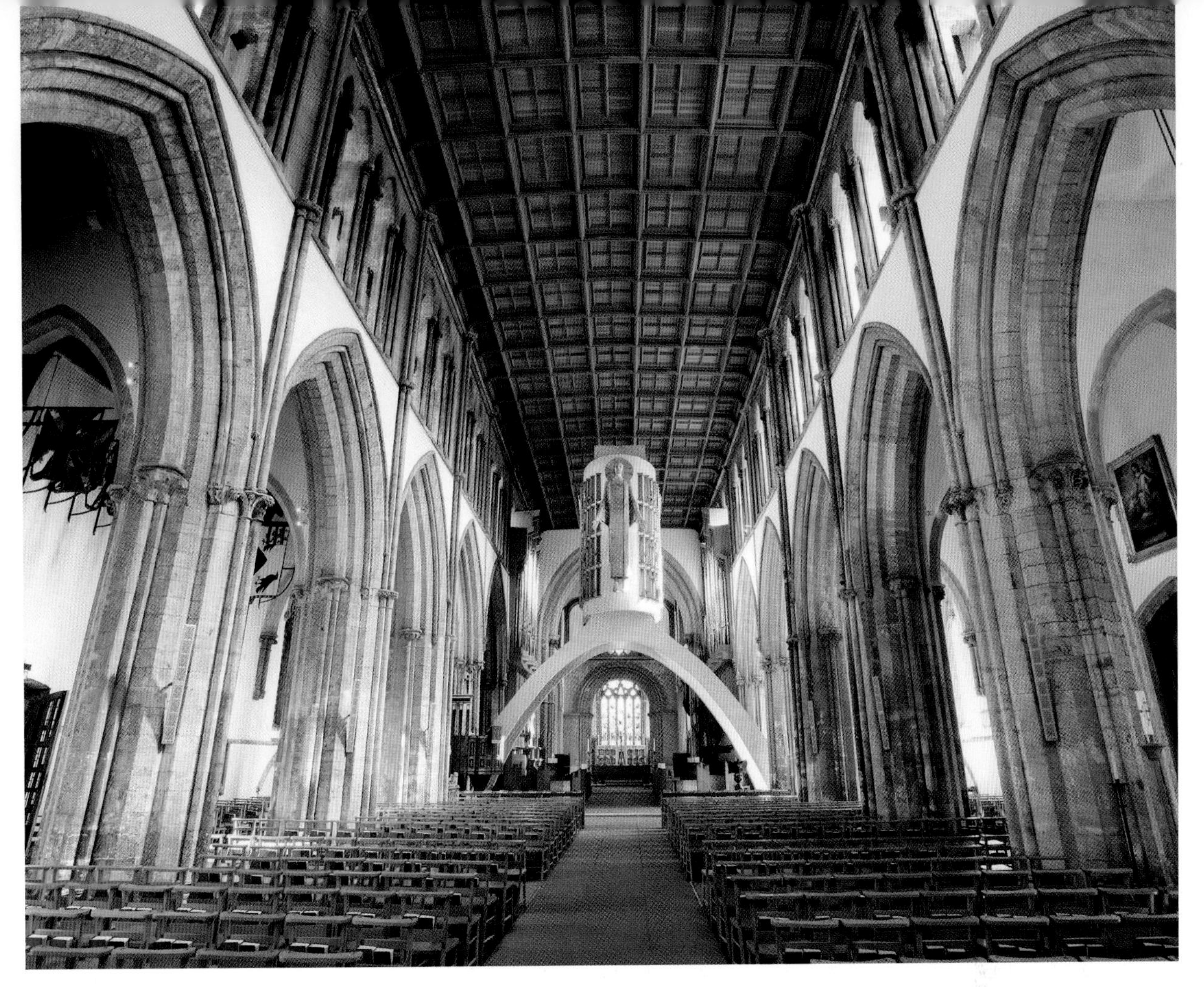

The nave with Jacob Epstein's Christ in Majesty.

following his victory at Bosworth Field ending the Wars of the Roses.

The sixteenth century marked the beginning of a period of great hardship for the cathedral. Along with other Welsh cathedrals, Llandaff suffered both during the Reformation and the Civil War. St Teilo's silver shrine was desecrated in 1548. Then, during the time of Cromwell's Commonwealth, in 1646, the building became the home of an ale bar, a cattle pen (in the choir), stables and a post office, causing further deterioration to the building. Both the south-west and north-west towers fell into disrepair and, around the turn of the eighteenth century, great storms wrought further damage.

In 1734 John Wood, the Elder, of Bath was commissioned to rebuild. His vision was of an Italianate building modelled on the Jerusalem Temple, which was entirely out of keeping with the Gothic church, and not all his intended work was completed. By the early part of the nineteenth century still more repair was essential and Wood's Italianate temple was demolished as, in 1841, T.H. Wyatt and John Prichard began a complete programme of restoration. Later in the nineteenth century, J.P. Seddon took responsibility for the building and it was he who invited members of the Pre-Raphaelite Brotherhood to design stained glass for the cathedral. Morris and Co. commissioned Dante Gabriel Rossetti, Ford Madox Brown and Edward Burne-Jones to make glass for the east window and for a series of windows at the entrance to the Chapter House.

Llandaff continued to face challenges well into the twentieth century when, in 1941, a German bomb destroyed much of the church. George Pace was the chosen architect for the rebuilding; he restored the Gothic structure but added nobly to the cathedral in building the new processional way and the David Chapel (a focus for the Welch Regiment) to the south west. Perhaps most daringly of all, he designed the amazing parabolic chancel arch upon which sits the Majestas, a figure of Christ in Majesty, surmounting the organ. Llandaff has become the focus for many significant events in the national life of Wales and further works of art, including Hicks-Jenkins' *Virgin of the Goldfinches*, have been commissioned. Llandaff Cathedral is a testimony to the endurance of the Christian faith in the face of great turmoil and suffering.

GLOSSARY

AISLE in a church, either the areas either side of the nave, separated from it by pillars, or a passage running between the rows of seats

AMBO a pulpit or raised reading stand in early Christian churches

AMBULATORY in a monastery, a cloister or place for walking. Often covered and making use of arcading

APSE a rounded recess with a domed roof, often situated at the end of the choir, aisles or nave of a church

ARCADING decoration by means of a series of arches

AUGUSTINIAN of the order of St Augustine of Hippo

AUMBRY locker or recess in a church wall in which sacramental vessels are stored

BALDACHINO a canopy, usually over an altar or a tomb, supported by columns

BARREL VAULT a vault with a semi-cylindrical roof

BAPTISTRY separate building containing the font

BASILICA a rectangular hall with two rows of columns and an apse at the end

BENEDICTINE of the order of St Benedict

BOSS an ornament fixed at the intersection of the arches which support a rib vault

BUTTRESS a structure built against a wall to support it, for example a flying buttress

CARMELITE of the order of Our Lady of Mount Carmel

CELLARER the officer of a monastery in charge of the cellar

CENSER a container in which incense is burned

CHANCEL the part of a church used by clergy and choir, to the east of the nave and transepts

CHANTRY a small chapel

CHAPTER HOUSE a building, often separate, used for meetings of a cathedral or monastic chapter

CHOIR OR QUIRE that part of a church where the church choir and clergy sit. Spelling alternates between entries depending on cathedral preferences.

CISTERCIAN an off-shoot of the Benedictine order, founded at Cîteaux in France in the late eleventh century

CLERESTORY the upper part of a large church, above the level of the roofs of the aisles, where windows let light into the central parts of the church

CLOISTERS covered passages connecting the church to other parts of a monastery

CLOSE the enclosed area around a cathedral

CORONA a crownlike chandelier

CROSSING the part of a cathedral where the nave intersects with the transept

CRYPT a subterranean cell, chapel or chamber that is usually vaulted

CURVILINEAR style of window design of the late Decorated period featuring flowing patterns of tracery

DECORATED architectural period (1307–77) which was characterised by the use of wider windows, projecting buttresses, tall pinnacles, and the rapid development of window tracery through the Geometric and Curvilinear styles

DOGTOOTH ornament on Early English arches

DOMINICAN of the order of St Dominic

DORTER a monastic dormitory

EARLY ENGLISH architecture of the earliest phase of the Gothic period

FAN-VAULTING a highly decorative and complex type of vaulting of the later Gothic period

FERETORY a shrine for relics used in procession

FLÈCHE a slim spire that rises from the point at which the nave and transepts intersect

FLYING BUTTRESS a prop built out from a pier or other support and supporting the main structure

FRANCISCAN of the order of St Francis of Assissi

FRONT in architecture, any side of a building, usually the one where the entrance is sited

GARTH an enclosed quadrangle surrounded by a cloister

GEOMETRIC a style of window design used in the early Decorated period centring on geometric shapes used mainly in the fourteenth century. It later developed into the more flowing Curvilinear style

GOTHIC architectural style prevalent in Western Europe from the twelfth to fifteenth centuries. It is characterised by the use of pointed archways

GRISAILLE a particular method of decorative painting on walls or ceilings

HOSTRY equivalent to 'hostelry' and related to 'hospital' and 'hotel', the word basically signifies a place where guests could stay

LANCET WINDOW high, narrow window with a pointed top

LIERNE rib vaulting of the Gothic period in which the ribs cross each other

MISERICORD a tip-up seat in a church with a projecting shelf on the underside, designed to support those standing at prayer for long periods

NARTHEX a vestibule between the cathedral entrance and the nave

NAVE the main part of a church, running from the main door to the choir in a west–east direction

NICHE a shallow recess in a wall for displaying a statue or other ornament

NIGHT STAIR staircase for monks to proceed from their dormitory into the choir for the overnight offices of Vigils and Prime

PERPENDICULAR architectural style (1377–1485), a phase of the Gothic period, when the designs of the Decorated period developed into longer, taller and more linear forms

PIER in architecture, a solid masonry support which sustains vertical pressure

PREACHING BOX a single-room church with a prominent pulpit made popular by Sir Christopher Wren after the Great Fire of London

PRESBYTERY the part of a church beyond the choir at the east end, where only the clergy would enter

PULPITUM a large stone or wooden screen or gallery between the nave and the choir

PYX the container in which the consecrated bread of the Eucharist is kept

QUATREFOIL in architecture, an ornament in the form of a ring of four leaves or petals

QUIRE see choir

REFECTORY the dining-room of a monastery

RELIQUARY a small box or shrine for holy relics (the mortal remains of saints)

REREDOS a decorative screen or painting behind the altar

RETABLE either a shelf for ornaments or a frame for decorative panels, found behind the altar of a church

RETRO-CHOIR OR RETRO-QUIRE the parts of a large church behind the high altar

RIB VAULT a vault built with 'ribs' or arches which support the roof

ROMANESQUE prevalent style of buildings erected in Europe between Roman times and the rise of Gothic style in the twelfth century

SEDILIA a canopied seat, or set of multiple seats, set into a recess in the south wall of the chancel, near the altar

SEE the city in which a bishop's church is located

SONG SCHOOL a room or rooms within a cathedral complex where choirs practice and music is kept

TRACERY ornamental stonework in Gothic windows

TRANSEPT the part of a cruciform church which crosses the nave in a north–south direction

TRANSITIONAL architecture of the period *c.* 1145–1190, when there was a gradual transition from Romanesque to Early Gothic

TRIFORIUM a gallery or arcade in the wall situated over the arches at the sides of the nave and choir

TURRET a small tower which forms part of the structure of a larger building

TYMPANUM the space between door lintel and arch

UNDERCROFT a crypt or vault below the floor of a church

VICARS CHORAL clergy or laymen appointed to sing services in the cathedral choir

INDEX

Winchester Cathedral's nave looking east.